Principles
to
Live By

Mel Rees

TEACH Services, Inc.
P U B L I S H I N G
www.TEACHServices.com • (800) 367-1844

Copyright © 2019 Mel Rees

Copyright © 2019 TEACH Services, 7 Inc.

ISBN-13: 978-1-4796-0879-9 (Paperback)

ISBN-13: 978-1-4796-0880-5 (ePub)

Library of Congress Control Number: 2019907450

TEACH Services, Inc.
P U B L I S H I N G
www.TEACHServices.com • (800) 367-1844

Table of Contents

Key to Abbreviations of E.G. White Book Titles

2T : *Testimonies for the Church*, Vol 2 (3T, 4T, 5T, etc.)

AH : *Adventist Home*

COL : *Christ's Object Lessons*

EW : *Early Writings*
LS : *Life Sketches*

MH : *Ministry of Healing*

MYP : *Messages to Young People*

PP : *Patriarchs and Prophets*

PK : *Prophets and Kings*

TM : *Testimonies to Ministers*

Introduction

Rules vs. Principles

The religious leaders in the time of Christ didn't consider Him a theologian. "How knoweth this man letters, having never learned?" (John 7:15). And in some circles today Jesus wouldn't be considered a theologian for the same reason.

His teaching astonished the doctors of the law for He did not deal in abstract theories. His instruction was practical—down to earth. It had to do with essential character development, the enlargement of a man's capacity to know God. He taught those principles which applied to daily living; those things that would once more unite man with the heavenly family.

God ordained that man should live by principle—not by rules. To obey a rule doesn't require any great degree of intelligence—all that is required is to do what the rule says ... and my dog can do that. He comes when I call—sits at my command. But to apply a principle requires intelligence of a higher order—mental and moral courage.

But, strange as it may seem, men would rather live by rules—it takes less effort—less thought—no decision.

Before sin entered the universe, there was only one principle, which was loving service. After the rebellion in heaven, there were two: loving service and selfishness. Because of this, God gave man some visual aids so he could better understand and apply the right principles.

The first full day man spent on this earth was the Sabbath. Often we think of the instruction "six days shalt thou labour," concerning the first six days of creation, but we should remember that for man the Sabbath came first. This was to teach the eternal principle that God must be *first*, first before our labor, first before every activity.

God specifically restricted the Tree of Knowledge of Good and Evil to teach man that he was a steward, not an owner. In absolute ownership there are no restrictions but in stewardship there is always some restriction.

The Ten Commandments which God gave on Mount Horeb were ten great principles given for the guidance and protection of his people. But the Israelites had lived by rules for well over one hundred years. The Egyptians made the rules and they either followed them-or else. Because of this, it was impossible for the Israelites to apply these principles to their daily activities, so God gave them the laws of Moses which were practical illustrations of these concepts.

But their religious leaders took these instructions and made rules out of them rather than applications of a principle. They dissected them and augmented them until by the time of Christ's first advent they covered every facet of life. There were intricate rules for Sabbath observance as well as tithe paying, for farming and business, and social intercourse. They were numerous and confusing.

Jesus tried to lead the people out of this theological and judicial jungle into the simplicity of living by principle. "Except your righteousness shall *exceed* the righteousness of the scribes and Pharisees," He said one time, "ye shall in no case enter into the kingdom of heaven" (Matt. 5:20; Italics supplied). The scribes and Pharisees had a righteousness but it was salvation by works.

Jesus pointed out the perpetuity of the law and condemned anyone who would tamper with it, then He pointed to some of the commandments and explained the depth and breadth of the principles involved. Thus He exposed the fatal mistake of the Jews in following an outward show of rules and regulations—but at the same time neglecting the principles involved.

For instance, He called attention to the commandment "Thou shalt not kill," and said that the principle was hatred. There are many ways to "kill" a person without taking his life. His life can be blighted and his productivity destroyed by gossip or slander.

The principle in the command, "Thou shalt not commit adultery," is lust. Jesus pointed out that the thought is equal to the deed.

On another occasion when asked which was *the* great commandment, He gave two cardinal principles: love for God and self-equating love for our neighbor. He said that all law is based on these two principles.

It is possible that the church today has been, or possibly still is guilty of emphasizing rules rather than principles. This could be due to the fact that people would rather follow rules than principles and leaders sometimes find it easier to make rules than teach principles. The pen of inspiration records this evaluation.

"The Word of God abounds in *general principles* for the formation of correct habits of living, and the Testimonies, general and personal, have been calculated to call their attention more especially to these principles" (4T, p. 323; Italics supplied).

To ministers this instruction was given:

"Those who have dwelt mostly upon the prophecies and theoretical points of our faith should without delay become Bible students upon *practical subjects.* They should take a *deeper draught* at the fountain of divine truth. They should carefully study the life of Christ and His *lessons of practical godliness"* (3T, p. 214; Italics supplied).

James defines "pure religion and undefiled" as a practical application of its principles (James 1:27). Ministering to the physical and spiritual needs of our fellow men constitutes acceptable service to God, according to Isaiah (Isa. 58:5–10).

In order to properly understand and appreciate the simplicity and beauty of living by principle, it is necessary to recognize the relationship between rules and principles as it relates to their differences.

- A rule, law, or requirement is a specific application of a principle which can be enforced. *It is impossible to enforce a principle.*

- A rule, law, or requirement is limited in scope and application For example, laws which apply to the people in one area may not apply to those in another. Diplomatic immunity allows certain people to do things forbidden to others. *A principle is universal and does not allow special privileges or diplomatic immunity.*

- A rule, law, or requirement is always subject to amendment or elimination. *A principle cannot be changed or discarded. Its only change is in its application to meet a specific situation.*

Situations Change—Principles Never Change

As stewards, we are endowed with mental, physical and moral capabilities. These must be developed and combined into an intangible we call character. This character is the only thing we will take, in its acceptable form, from this earth to the next. Therefore, these capabilities must be perfected through the power of choice— the choice and application, decision and implementation that form the foundation and growth of character.

It was to this end that God formed man a free, moral agent—a person who could recognize his capabilities and develop them to the glory of his Creator; a person who would be able to return love as he was loved. Such men were to take their places in the heavenly family as contributors to the celestial happiness.

To accomplish this divine purpose, a man must recognize his origin and his God-given appointment as a manager over the things with which he has been entrusted. Dominion calls for individual decision and action—therefore, God gave man great, guiding principles to live by.

Keep it Simple

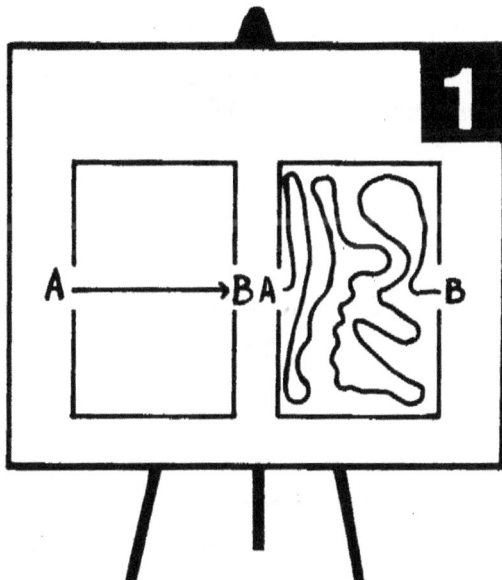

One of the strange results of all human activity is that it rarely remains simple. A small group will band together for a common cause or objective—then, sooner or later, they will become a club, an association, or a society complete with officers, bylaws, payrolls, committees, and scheduled meetings, many of which are productive of no more good than just having them.

Small communities end up as cities—tribes, as nations, with complex governments requiring and spending vast sums for structural maintenance. The amazing fact is that they never seem to decentralize—just eventually collapse from their unwieldiness.

Even the church is not immune. People of like beliefs and common objectives, seeking to expand their activities, eventually end up in the maze of an organizational structure. Too often this becomes so complicated that its leaders barely recognize the desires and needs of the constituents, isolated as they are by the policies and machinery of the structure.

It must be recognized, however, that organization is essential to the accomplishment of any major undertaking. Factories, public works, hospitals, etc., are dependent on some base of support. And worldwide missionary programs would never be successful without a firm structure to guide and support them.

But the side effects so often seen in organization must be a matter of some concern, for the dangers of over-structuring are always present and the time could come when the structure will exist solely for its own support and its mission will become only the byproduct of its existence.

Religion has always been a fertile field for consolidation and confederation. It is so easy to get caught in the net of goals, objectives, policies and procedures that the very simplicity of the gospel may be lost sight of or considered too elementary. Even religion can be departmentalized and secularized to the extent that it loses its sense of mission and becomes an end in itself.

Paul was concerned about this. "But I fear, lest by any means, as the serpent beguiled Eve through his subtlety, so your minds should be corrupted from the *simplicity* that is in Christ" (II Cor. 11:3; Italics supplied). The simplicity of Jesus Christ is in the principles which He taught as the basis of His kingdom.

For example, He gave a principle which would guarantee harmony between individuals in their relationships with each other. "Therefore all things whatsoever ye would that men should do to you, do ye even so to them" (Matt. 7:12).

But this is too simple. We like to make it complicated—so we study psychology and sociometry, get degrees and hold seminars on human relationships, complete with long lists of "what to do" and "what not to do."

But seminars breed seminars and we find ourselves like the woman who came to Jesus who had spent all her money seeking medical help—and worse off than before. Evidence shows that we are no nearer solving the problems of human relationship than we ever were because we are trying to follow a set of rules of conduct rather than a principle of divine origin.

Even as simple a truth as the relationship between the *law* and *grace* is often buried under an avalanche of theological theory and vocabulary when it is so simple a child can understand it. Notice the relationship in this simple diagram.

In the beginning God created the world. He made a man and gave him dominion over the world. Man was a steward and there was one restriction in his dominion—the Tree of Knowledge of Good and Evil. This tree which God did not prevent Adam from touching guaranteed him the power of choice. This gave the lie to the devil's claim that God was a dictator forcing His subjects to serve Him.

Now the *law* stated that if the man violated the restriction in his stewardship he would die. This was not unreasonable, for a violation of the restriction in management is theft or embezzlement and the penalties for these crimes have always been severe. Refusing to recognize God's ownership would constitute anarchy or rebellion and no government can tolerate this.

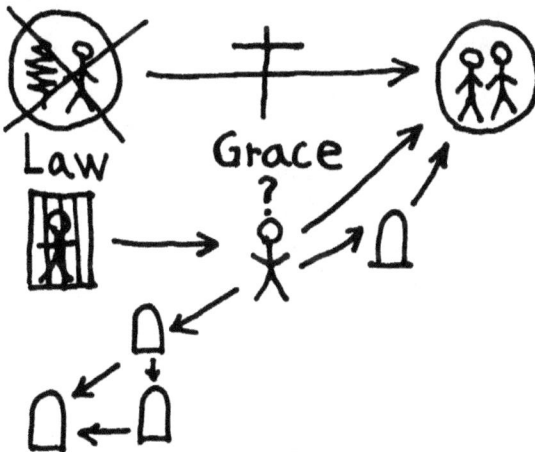

Man broke the law and doomed the entire human race to eternal death. From that day to this every person has been born on death row: "For all have sinned ... the wages of sin is death" (Rom. 5:12; 6:23).

But God loved the man He created so much that He made provision that man might not have to die eternally. This provision was made through His Son who satisfied the claims of the law and made it possible for man to once more have the power of choice. This was undeserved *grace*.

Now each individual stands where Adam stood with the privilege to choose life or death, heaven or hell. It is his choice.

Through *grace* man is taken from death row and is faced with two choices. He can take the single-tombstone route and go to heaven; or he can take the double-tombstone route and be eternally lost. Someone will remember Enoch and Elijah who went to heaven without seeing death also those who will be alive at His second coming. But, things always balance out for there are those who will die three times! "Behold, he cometh with clouds; and every eye shall see him, and *they also which pierced him*" (Rev. 1:7; Italics supplied).

Those who "pierced him" are now dead. They will be raised to see Him come in the clouds, they will then die again but will be resurrected at the coming of the New Jerusalem from heaven, then die eternally.

Think of the law and grace in this hypothetical case. A man commits a capital crime. He is caught, tried, convicted and sentenced to die. This is the *law*. But the governor through *grace* pardons him and he is now free. His freedom will stand as long as he obeys the law. Grace never gives license to sin, only pardons the sinner who is already guilty under the law.

How desperately we need to understand the simplicity of the gospel. When we make it complicated, it is so difficult to understand and put into practice.

Throughout His ministry, Jesus tried to present the principles which relate to His kingdom, but His hearers were so obsessed with the idea that He came to establish a temporal kingdom, with its offices and organization, that most of His teaching fell on deaf ears. His work always appeared to be on the edge of apparent failure. Only after it appeared that His mission had utterly collapsed did His followers begin to understand what He was trying to tell them.

The principles of His kingdom were unrestricted love for God with a corresponding love for our neighbor. As members of the heavenly family, we would treat ourselves and each other with loving courtesy. The principle of love would direct every thought and action. This was His message—but maybe it was too simple.

Steward or Slave

It is strange that only in the Christian community is the term stewardship misunderstood. In a time when many people are searching for their "roots" it must be the devil's studied plan to equate stewardship with money so men will not see that it is really a relationship.

Our "roots" can be found in Genesis 1:26: "Let us make man in our image, after our likeness: and let them have dominion." We are born stewards.

A steward has control over the goods entrusted to him while a slave's life and property are under the absolute control of another person. Because God gave each of us the power of choice, we can either be His stewards or slaves to the devil, and there is no alternative.

STEWARDSHIP IS THE USE OF TIME, ABILITIES, AND POSSESSIONS—ENTRUSTED BUT NOT OWNED.

In order for a Christian to have meaning and direction to his life, he must understand not only his origin but also the tools with which he has to work.

First, he is given a measure of time. Time is the substance of life. Each person has been given the same amount of time during the period of his responsibility. A loss of time is a loss of life. When a person is imprisoned, he loses a portion of his life.

Each person has been given ample time for the duties of life and preparation for the future one. How he uses this time determines his success or failure. Solomon said, "To every thing there is a season, and a time to every purpose under the heaven" (Eccles. 3:1).

Second, everyone is given ability, or abilities. These vary according to the capacity to use them. Jesus spoke of this distribution in His parable of the talents "unto one he gave five talents, to another two, and to another one; to every man according to his several ability" (Matt. 25:15). There is something unique about this distribution of abilities.

EVERY PERSON IN THE WORLD CAN EXCEL EVERY OTHER PERSON IN SOMETHING.

This simply means that one can take any two people from any period of the world—and each one will excel the other in something!

In Africa there is a very primitive tribe who have no permanent homes, but who have the ability to paint the most beautiful pictures of animals on the sandstone cliffs. Even if there were those who could equal or excel them in this painting, would these same artists be able to track an animal across the desert, not allowing it to eat, drink, or rest, until they could kill it with a short spear? Likely not.

Recognizing the fact that each person possesses an ability greater than our own will prevent personal pride from causing us to depreciate *any* of our fellow men.

There is possibly another reason why God gave his stewards different abilities: it makes them dependent on each other. The needs of one must be supplied by the skills of another. This mutual dependence will draw them together into a brotherhood, as the family of God.

It is a law of abilities that they increase as they are used and decrease if unused. Their greatest increase will be seen when they are employed to bless others. When selfishly employed, "they diminish and are finally withdrawn" (COL, p. 364).

The steward is responsible for his talents and will be held accountable. "So then every one of us shall give account of himself to God" (Rom. 14.12). This responsibility and resultant accountability apply to each individual no matter whether he chooses to be a steward of God or a slave to the devil.

THE WISE USE OF OUR TIME AND TALENTS WILL RESULT IN POSSESSIONS.

These possessions increase the responsibility and accountability for they equip a person for a total stewardship.

However, even though a person may then be fully equipped for action, there is another requirement—divine power.

An automobile may have body, motor, tires and fuel, but without the spark it will go nowhere. So the steward needs the divine "spark," divine power, to function at all.

IN EVERYTHING THAT TENDS TO THE SUSTENANCE OF MAN IS SEEN THE CONCURRENCE OF DIVINE POWER AND HUMAN EFFORT.

A friend of mine was telling of a neighbor who had recently returned from exploring some old Indian ruins. They found a room, high on the cliff, that had been undisturbed for several centuries. In it they found primitive tools, furniture, cooking utensils—and a covered pot of dried beans. He brought some of the beans home— planted them—and they grew! After centuries in that pot.

I couldn't control my eagerness. "You must get me some of those beans," I pleaded.

"I don't know if I can."

"But you must."

"Okay," he shrugged, "I'll try."

"Don't *try*," I urged. "Just get them!"

I watched every mail. Then, one day there was a small package and in it nine purplish beans! I was elated. In a sunny spot in the garden, I planted those nine beans.

Every day I watched that little plot of ground. Then one beautiful morning I saw a little "fiddle neck" breaking through the soil—then another—and another until all nine of them reached for the sun.

How carefully I tended those beans! I even cut some long poles and arranged them "tepee fashion" (since they were Indian beans I thought this would make them happy). I hoed and weeded and they grew—up, up they climbed. What fantastic blooms—what huge pods—what beautiful beans. What a spiritual lesson!

God didn't plant them. I did. But I couldn't give them life. He did. He didn't hoe and weed them. I did. But I couldn't furnish the sunshine and rain. He did.

GOD AND I ARE PARTNERS!

This beautiful concept can be illustrated by the following diagram. The most fully equipped steward is limited in capacity, but God is unlimited. Therefore, a steward's potential can be measured by this scale.

THE CAPACITY USE OF TIME, ABILITIES, AND POSSESSIONS *PLUS* DIVINE POWER EQUAL HIS POTENTIAL.

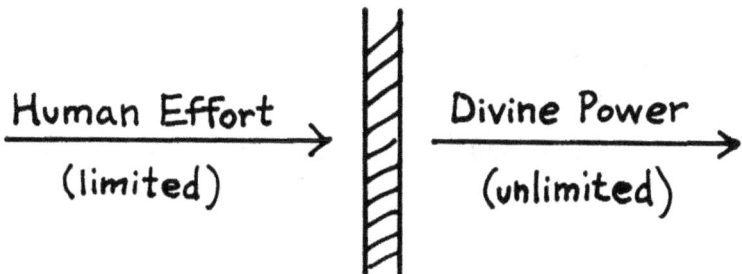

$$\underrightarrow{\text{Human Effort}}_{\text{(limited)}} \qquad \underrightarrow{\text{Divine Power}}_{\text{(unlimited)}}$$

The man had such a serious speech defect that it was some time before I could make out what he was trying to say. I finally figured out that he wouldn't be able to join our visitation program for people wouldn't be able to understand him. This was evident.

Only the Lord could have impressed me to say in reply, "Of course, if God wanted you to visit, He would place an interpreter between you and the people you are visiting and they would understand clearly whatever you said." Strangely enough, I promptly forgot the incident. I was getting so I could understand much of what he said, and he was a very successful visitor. I just didn't think about it anymore.

Eighteen months later, we were having a meeting of some of the men in the church at his home. At the conclusion of the meeting, I prepared to leave. I remember it was a cold night and I had forgotten to take a topcoat. When he followed me out of the house, I secretly hoped he wouldn't detain me for I was looking forward to the warmth of the car heater.

He didn't seem to notice the cold and I waited for a few chilling moments before he spoke.

"The other day," he began, "a lady came to visit my wife. She told her that she and her family 'date' their Christian experience to the night I visited them over a year ago. She said that I explained the work of the church and God's program so beautifully that they just fell in love with God."

As I was thinking and wondering, he continued.

"I thought you would like to know for you are responsible."

"How am I responsible?" I asked.

"Don't you remember the night I told you I couldn't visit because no one would understand me, and you said if God wanted me to visit He would send an interpreter to explain what I said?"

"Oh, yes, I do remember."

"Well, I prayed—and felt impressed to visit—and now you can see the result."

"But that's wonderful," I replied. I was too filled with wonder to say anything more. I realized that this was indeed a miracle. He didn't make any move to return to the house and I'll confess I wasn't conscious of the cold anymore.

At length, he said, "That isn't all. One day I was sitting in church and as I looked around I couldn't see one soul that was there because of me. The thought crossed my mind that I wouldn't enjoy heaven unless there was *one* soul that I had gotten—all by myself. So I began to pray for this one soul.

"One day I went to see a lady about some repair work she wanted on her house. She was concerned about some happenings in her area when some toughs from the city had caused a lot of damage. She asked me when I thought it would all end. I told her that would be when Jesus came, as it says in the Bible."

"Does it say that in the Bible?" she asked.

"That's right," I told her. "Haven't you read the Bible?"

"No, I never read it."

"Would you like to study the Bible?"

"I surely would."

"When would you like to begin?"

"How about Sunday night?"

So, he said that now he had found the soul—he needed someone who would give her Bible studies. But Sunday the pastor would be out of town so that was out. He contacted several other members of the church but they all had appointments. Finally, he realized that *he* was going to have to give the Bible study Sunday night—and he had never given one!

Saturday evening he alternately studied, prayed and wept. Finally, he went to bed exhausted. All day Sunday he studied, prayed and wept. It was no use—he just couldn't do it. When seven o'clock came, he felt he must go to apologize to her, anyway.

He said he stopped his car outside her house and prayed, "Lord, I have feet—they'll get me inside…but Lord, she'll never understand what I say—You'll have to take care of that."

He said he didn't have to ring the bell— *"She could hear my knees knocking!"*

I waited as he paused—then quietly, almost reverently, he added, "Last month she was baptized."

"That's wonderful," I managed to say but I was too choked up to say anything else.

After a moment or two, he continued.

"I have a man, his wife, and two children who are going to be baptized next month." Now I couldn't say anything.

This man's brother-in-law tells me that when he goes to visit him, it takes at least a half day before he can carry on a reasonable conversation. But such is the potential of a Christian when he combines human effort with divine power.

Seek First

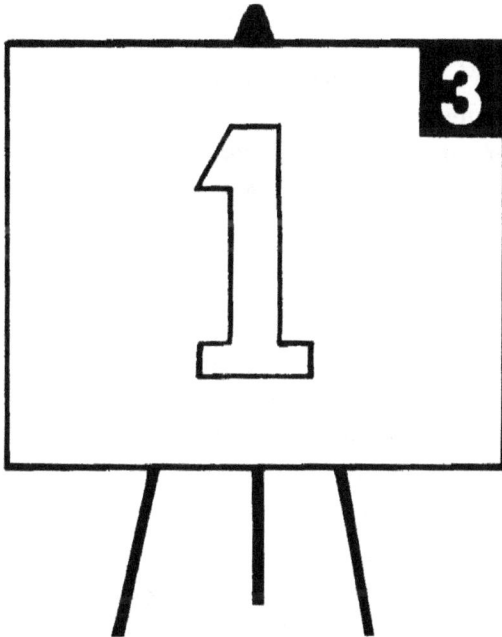

The Christian steward will need guidance and direction. This will be found in the principles of the Bible and put in the framework of a practical application in the Spirit of Prophecy. Jesus emphasized *the* great principle of life when He said, "But seek ye first the kingdom of God, and His righteousness; and all these things shall be added unto you" (Matt. 6:33).

This text, so well known, often quoted, is rarely understood and more rarely practiced. The key word is *first*. There are many people who seek the kingdom of God, but rarely, if ever, is it first.

Jesus did not say we were not to seek other things such as happiness, security, educational attainments, or even financial objectives. What He did say was that these things must be secondary; we must seek the kingdom of God *first*.

What was the setting for this strange, impractical statement?

He was holding a seminar for His disciples. They had recently been ordained. He led them to the seaside where He was going to try to correct their erroneous ideas regarding His mission.

They were so obsessed with the concept of a temporal kingdom in which they would hold all the important positions that they failed to correctly interpret His messages and actions. Somehow, Jesus felt that after witnessing His works and listening to His teaching, possibly now they would understand.

Before He could begin to teach them, however, vast crowds of people began to gather. He realized that they would be unable to hear Him in the narrow confines of the seashore, so He led the way to the side of a nearby mountain.

They were all there, not only the local folks but also those from all the surrounding areas. There were peasants, farmers, fishermen, Jewish rulers, and Roman soldiers. It was a cross-section of society from the very rich to the very poor.

They had come for many reasons: some from curiosity, many to be healed, some from skepticism, hundreds to join the revolution. Many were seeking something better than their drab, uninteresting lives; but there was a common denominator which characterized the entire group—each one was searching for a material solution to a material problem. That's why this "seek first" message must have been such a shock to them.

Jesus didn't attack their errors, He simply outlined the principles of His kingdom and let them draw their own conclusions. One can imagine their surprise when He said, "Blessed are the poor." They probably didn't hear the "in spirit" part—the word poor would create an immediate block in their thinking. What is so blessed about being poor, or meek or merciful? This isn't what they came to hear. They anticipated some announcement that would signal the end of their domination by the Romans. This would really cause them to shout with joy. But their harsh life under the Romans wasn't the problem.

These were strange philosophies—not what they were used to hearing. Some probably scoffed, others wondered. Then it appears that in pity for their wretched condition (the rich who had everything and were still dissatisfied, and the poor who had nothing and were envious of those who did) He began to speak of the very necessities of life—food, shelter, and clothing.

But Jesus reminded them that these were the goals of heathen people. "You have a heavenly Father who loves you," He told them, "He knows what you need and will provide these things for you…if you will only seek Him first." But this was such a strange, impractical approach to the problems of life. What could it all mean?

Their religious leaders could have told them, if they wanted to. They were always quoting Moses. They knew that in the beginning God provided everything man would ever desire or need. He gave him dominion over a world of unsurpassed beauty, teeming with life, bustling with activity. This man was given not only dominion over all the earth, but also the *freedom of dependence.*

We usually think of freedom as related to independence, but this wasn't God's plan. Consider for a moment. Adam and Eve had no clothing problems, no health, employment, housing or social problems. That was real freedom.

When they bartered their freedom of dependence for the so-called freedom of independence which the devil promised them, they immediately lost their home. They had clothing problems and there was a change in the weather. Now they had to earn their living by the sweat of hard labor; briars and thorns scratched them. Eve knew pain for the first time as she bore her children—and they needed health insurance and death benefits!

They really didn't make too sharp a deal that day down in the orchard!

When God brought Israel into Canaan, He gave them a plan for social and economic security which would guarantee them health and prosperity. Deuteronomy 8 presents a veritable utopia.

Everything was provided for their use and enjoyment. But this "seek first" principle was paramount to the plan. Only by following it would they be able to enjoy the *freedom of dependence* which God promised.

The first that ripened of every product was consecrated to Him. The first of the flocks and herds, the firstborn son. All these were to be a constant reminder that God was the Owner and they were only tenant farmers, stewards.

One might think that these requirements, which touched every aspect of their lives, would eventually reduce them to poverty; but on the contrary, they were *the* condition for their prosperity. You see, God promised them freedom from disease, abundant crops, health, happiness and the right amount of rain at *the right time*.

But they couldn't stand prosperity and they traded their freedom of dependence on God for the gods of the Amorites, the Hittites, and the Moabites. They discarded the "seek first" principle and spent seventy years living by the *rules* of the Babylonians.

They never seemed to learn. The first lesson God had to teach them when they returned from captivity was the "seek first" principle.

One can imagine they reasoned this way. When we get our farms into production, rebuild our houses, and get a little money in the bank—then we'll start thinking about building a church. It may have been logical but it did not comply with the principle that God must be first.

"Is it time for you, O ye, to dwell in your cieled houses, and this house lie waste?" (Hag. 1:4). Then God told them they should consider. No matter how hard they worked, they didn't produce much. Their pocketbooks were full of holes and when they did manage to bring some money home, He said He "blew upon it."

They were instructed to begin God's house and on the very day they began to build He began to bless them. Only by making God first would they be successful.

I remember having dinner in a lovely home on a hill overlooking a beautiful valley and hearing a modern version of this experience as related by Haggai.

My host, a truck driver, and his wife had purchased a lot a few years prior to this, and were saving money to build a home. As I recall, they had saved six thousand dollars when the little church to which they belonged decided to build a new one. They really needed one for the present building wasn't representative at all. This did present a problem, however.

This couple had to decide which was more important—God's house—or their own. They prayed over the matter and applying the "seek first" principle placed the entire six thousand dollars in the building fund!

Within two weeks of this decision, the company where he worked had such an increase in business they had to buy a new truck to handle it. This would entail lots of overtime (with extra pay) and he volunteered to drive it.

He said he never made money so fast in his life. One time he was stranded in a faraway city for two weeks because of bad weather and drew double time around the clock!

It took four years to dedicate the new church free from debt. On the day the church was dedicated their lovely home on the hill was also built—and free from debt! "There is no way," he told me, "that we could have built this house and paid for it under normal circumstances, it was a miracle of God." Two weeks after the house was built, the business dropped off—the company sold the extra truck.

There are many who don't think this "seek first" principle will work in today's materialistic, mixed-up world. But what other solution is there?

A study of the world's history will reveal that in every age, in every society there have been the same problems. Programs without number have been designed to solve these problems without any success. Jesus said, "Seek ye first the kingdom of God" and *it is the only solution the world has never tried!*

The Christian steward can have the *freedom of dependence* because Jesus obligated His Father that day on the hills of Galilee. "All these things will be provided," He promised, "if you will. ..."

And to everyone who accepts this eternal principle He left a legacy of peace. In a time when the world overflows with moral corruption, poverty, crime and economic uncertainty, the Christian can have the peace and the freedom of dependence, because he has, as Jesus pointed out, a heavenly Father who loves Him. But he must "seek first."

Fear and/or Unbelief

It began with gunfire in the night and the shout: "Don't shoot him in the head!" The woman grabbed her twelve-year-old daughter and fled into the woods.

For two weeks they ran through the forest, living off berries and roots and at night covering themselves with dirt as they slept. They managed to stay a step ahead of the men searching for them, whom they believed had killed ten of their fellow campers, including the woman's husband and son.

Their terror was real, but there were no murders, and the searchers thought they had been kidnapped. What did happen?

Authorities said that some camp officials were merely killing a raccoon so it could be tested for rabies following the biting of another camper earlier in the week. Then there were some fireworks set off in the area at the same time as the piercing shout, "Don't shoot him in the head."

Thus began a two-week search for mother and daughter who remained quietly hidden every time their rescuers got near. Finally, exhausted and nearly naked, they stumbled onto a forest access road where a passing motorist picked them up and returned them to safety.

Fear is a broad term we use to describe a particular feeling. Because of its dual nature and degrees of intensity, we use specific terms such as dread, worry, apprehension and anxiety. Fright is sudden, violent alarm. Horror is extreme fear, while terror is uncontrolled fear.

Fear is common to birds, fish, animals, and man. Of these, only man has the capacity to deal with fear intelligently.

Fear had its origin in disobedience. Adam and Eve had eaten of the forbidden fruit and they heard the voice of God in the garden. The Bible says they were afraid (Gen. 3:10). Since that fateful day, fear has been the unwelcome companion of every individual.

Because of its dual nature, fear can either be a protector or a destroyer. Because of the fear of fire, hundreds of people have been killed, not because of the fire, but because they panicked and jammed the exit doors. On the other hand, because of this same fear we take precautions against fire and warn children not to touch hot stoves.

Here are some observations regarding fear.

- It always relates to the future (if we fear the past, it is because we are afraid that something we have done will be found out—which still puts it in the future).
- Fear is not a private affair (one person deeply affected can affect others).
- Fear cannot stand constructive action (present action generates future security).

Most adults are conditioned to fear in childhood. Placing a child in a dark room may lead to fear of the dark. Playfully shoving him toward the edge of a cliff can lead to acrophobia.

I confess to a touch of claustrophobia dating back to my childhood, when on my way home from school, I crawled into a culvert under the road—and got stuck! I managed to wiggle out but the fright it gave me taught me to stay out of culverts.

Years later, while crawling under the house to repair something, my shoulders were caught between two timbers and momentarily I felt that same sensation of panic I had felt in the culvert.

Because fear can so seriously affect our lives and the lives of others, parents should treat all childhood fears with seriousness, gentleness and understanding. They should help a child weed out those fears which are purely imaginative from those which can be constructive.

The Christian must clearly understand fear in both its positive and negative nature. The fear of the Lord is a great motivating force; fearing to follow His directions can lead to disaster.

A study of the nature of fear is also important for it has a twin sister which is unbelief. And while unbelief is the requisite for fear—fear can also be the requisite for unbelief. The story of the Israelites provides abundant proof for this.

First, there was the fear of the Red Sea while Pharaoh's cavalry thundered down on them. Then they didn't believe God could provide them with food and water in the desert for forty years. Right on the borders of Canaan, after being provided with everything they needed all those years, they didn't believe God when their water supply was cut off and they had to detour all the way around the land of Edom when they might have passed directly through it to Canaan, which was God's plan.

They never really believed or trusted God because of fear and fear caused their unbelief.

If the "seek first" principle is the answer to all of life's problems, why doesn't everyone accept and follow it? The answer is that they don't believe. People just don't believe that in a practical, day-by-day existence, a person can make God first and still survive. Why?

THE DEVIL LAYS THE SEED OF UNBELIEF BY SUBSTITUTING REASON FOR FAITH.

While God expects His stewards to use their reasoning powers, reason must acknowledge an authority which is superior to itself. One must recognize that God isn't subject to human limitations, either in planning or action. A creator would hardly be limited by his works. But there is a limitation.

WE ARE LIMITED TO *FOLLOWING DIRECTIONS—* GOD IS UNLIMITED IN PRODUCING THE RESULTS.

Fear of the future has always been one of the devil's most potent weapons to counteract faith. Of *modern* Israel it is said: "They *fear* that they may come to want, or that their children may become needy, or that their grandchildren will be destitute. They dare not trust God" (2T, p. 657; Italics supplied).

This sounds strangely familiar. When the spies returned from Canaan with the report that there were giants in the land, the people cried, "Wherefore hath the Lord brought us unto this land, to fall by the sword, that our *wives* and our *children* should be a prey? were it not better for us to return to Egypt?" (Num. 14:3; Italics supplied). There doesn't seem to be much difference between ancient and modern Israel, after all.

Fear will also figure prominently in the final conflict between good and evil. The devil, in consultation with his angels, was overheard to say: "I will make the observance of the seventh day a sign of disloyalty to the authorities of the earth. Human laws will be made so stringent that men and women will not dare to observe the seventh-day Sabbath. *For fear of wanting food and clothing*, they will join with the world in transgressing God's law" (PK, p. 184; Italics supplied).

Satan will not fully succeed in his plan for there will be those who love and trust God and won't be afraid for their food and clothing. "There is no fear in love; but perfect love casteth out fear" (I John 4:18).

It was a stormy night on Galilee. The winds were so strong that little ship was being tossed from wave to wave. Suddenly, the disciples saw Jesus walking on the water. Peter, good, old impetuous Peter, said, "Bid me come to thee *on the water*" (Matt. 14:28; Italics supplied). And Jesus said, "Come."

Peter was doing all right, *walking on water*, until he suddenly remembered that the winds were "boisterous" and he shouldn't be out there. He was immediately afraid and began to sink. He cried out, "Lord, save me." And Jesus reached out and caught him, saying, "O thou of little faith, wherefore didst thou doubt?" (vs. 31).

When reason tells us the Lord's plans won't work, or when we are up against a hard place in our daily lives, right then Jesus is ready to stretch out His hand, if we will only cry, "Lord, save me."

IT IS WHEN WE ARE DEEPLY TROUBLED—WHEN THE OUTLOOK IS DARKEST THAT DIVINE HELP IS THE NEAREST.

Fear and unbelief entered the world with sin and they will exit together: "But the *fearful*, and *unbelieving*, and the abominable, and murderers, and whoremongers, and sorcerers, and idolaters, and all liars, shall have their part in the lake which burneth with fire and brimstone" (Rev. 21:8; Italics supplied).

It seems so strange that a lot of honest, moral, church-going folks may find themselves in the company of all these horrible people just because they are fearful and unbelieving, or unbelieving and fearful, whichever comes first.

Jesus didn't say there wouldn't be things to cause fear. In fact, He said that conditions on the earth would be so terrible that men's hearts would fail them for fear. But to His followers He directed, "And when these things begin to come to pass, then look up, and lift up your heads; for your redemption draweth nigh" (Luke 21:28).

We have been told: "We have nothing to fear for the future except as we shall forget how the Lord has led us, and His teaching in our past history" (LS, p. 196).

Our prayer should be like that of the distraught father who brought his son to Jesus to be healed. When he was asked if he believed, he answered, "Lord, I believe, help Thou mine unbelief."

We have nothing to fear for the future except....

Fringe Areas

If it hadn't been so late and the caller's voice so desperate, I am sure I would have refused outright. It did seem like a simple request—conduct the week of prayer for some third-graders—but my experience and specialty didn't involve this age group, and besides I had been conditioned early in my ministry to avoid this sort of confrontation. It happened like this.

It was my first camp meeting as a minister and I was asked to tell a campfire story to some juniors. I really couldn't refuse, being newly arrived and all, so I agreed.

Imagine my consternation when I found I was to follow one of the denomination's most famous storytellers! My mind said to run—but my feet refused.

All I can say is that I did the best I could. Using all the enthusiasm at my command (which was woefully inadequate, I am sure) I told, what was to me at least, a thrilling story. Right at the climactic part, I asked, "Now what do you think happened?" And a boy said, "How do we know...you're telling the story." And I died inside and vowed *no junior stories* ... ever!

It seemed the one who had been chosen to conduct these meetings was ill and the caller was desperate. (He had to be, I thought, to call me.) Because the first meeting was at eight thirty the following morning I didn't have time to panic, or recover from it, if I had. I felt somehow the Lord would see me through and frankly it was a delightful experience, I found, to my surprise, a roomful of eager youngsters under the perfect control of a teacher who somehow didn't seem to....

I freely confess that I followed the Biblical injunction about taking no thought for the morrow because I went to the first appointment without an idea in my head. Somehow, the Lord always provided.

I managed to survive day one, two, and three. On the morning of the fourth day I was driving to the school wondering as usual what I was going to talk about, when I began to wonder if these youngsters knew what a fringe area was. They didn't—but it seemed like such a good idea I determined to find some means to explain it to them. (Besides, what else was there!)

Everyone encounters fringe areas in the decisions of life—grey areas, they are sometimes called. These fringe or grey areas are those activities in which neither the rules of right nor the rules of wrong seem to apply. Often one hears the question, "What's wrong with it?" and there isn't a concrete answer because there are so many variables.

In the center of the fringe area is a tightrope. The devil would like for us to walk this narrow strand for he knows that if we walk it long enough eventually we will fall off.

Scientific tests show that a person walking a rail will always fall off on the right side, if he is righthanded. He will more often fall on the left if he is lefthanded. But, if one walks the tight-wire between right and wrong long enough, he will eventually lose his balance and fall—*always on the wrong side!*

Because of this, it is imperative that a Christian understand the principle involved with fringe areas and how to cope with it.

To get this principle across to my third-graders I asked them to give me a list of things they knew were right. I wrote these on the board as fast as they gave them. Then we made a list of things that were wrong. As they watched intently, I drew the picture of a bare fishhook and asked if they would put this on a line to go fishing. "Oh, no!" quickly spoke up one little fellow.

"Why not?" I asked.

"Because the fish would see the hook," he answered.

"All right," I said, "how about this?" And I drew a tail on the hook, a fuzzy body, some wings, and feet. "Now, how about this beautiful little bug—would they bite this?" A little girl thought it would be all right, but my little expert emphatically said that it wouldn't work for the fish could still see the hook

"But aren't you forgetting something?"

"I don't know." He looked puzzled.

"You must remember that the fish is on the bottom of the stream and the fly is on top of the water. From where he is, the fly seems to be floating on a mirror and he can't see the hook at all for it is *underneath*. As he watches this bug floating along, he doesn't see anything wrong, so he bites it and suddenly finds he has made a big mistake—there's a hook in it!"

The little girls gasped but my little fishing expert had a smug smile on his face, no doubt thinking more about the fellow holding the fishing pole than the hapless plight of the fish.

Now I asked them what things they could think of that might have hooks in them. I explained that Satan is a smart fisherman and is very clever in concealing hooks so we won't see them. To give them an idea to start, I wrote the word "B-O-O-K-S" and asked if books were good or bad.

"Bad!" explained my little fisherman, which left no doubt in my mind regarding his love for school versus the woods and streams near his home. (I still wonder how that teacher got such perfect deportment from him.)

Most of the answers regarding books were *good* but one little girl said there were bad books, such as novels and the like. We agreed that books could have *Satan's hooks* in them and we'd best be careful what we read.

There are "hooks" even in books that are considered good because they have either a good moral or tell of a conversion experience following a recital of the sordid details of a misspent life.

"Books that delineate the Satanic practice of human beings are giving *publicity to evil* works. The horrible details of crime and misery need not be lived over, and none should act a part in perpetuating their memory" (7T, p. 165). "The widespread use of such books at this time is one of the cunning devices of Satan" (MH, p. 447).

> The disposition to flatter and exalt those who have been rescued from the lowest depths sometimes proves their ruin. The practice of inviting men and women to relate in public the experience of their life of sin is full of danger to both speaker

and hearers. To dwell upon scenes of evil is corrupting to mind and soul. And the prominence given to the rescued ones is harmful to them. Many are led to feel that their sinful life has given them a certain distinction. A love of notoriety and a spirit of self-trust are encouraged that prove fatal to the soul. (MH, p. 178)

This discussion about books seemed to prime the pump and I asked for another suggestion.

"Music," said a little girl.

"Good or bad?" I asked.

As usual, I drew both answers and drew arrows pointing to both good and bad. But, one *bad* was so emphatic that I sought out the girl who said it and asked, "Honey, why did you say bad?"

She answered, "Rock and roll."

"Where do they play that?" I questioned.

"In my house!" was her emphatic reply.

"And you think that's bad?"

"Yes," she insisted. And I agreed with her.

I wonder how many of us past the third grade realize how easy it has been for the devil to put "hooks" in some of our music. "It is one of Satan's most attractive agencies to ensnare souls" (MYP, p. 295). All he has to do is set beautiful Christian themes to country or disco music and the trap is baited. If one walks this "tight rope" long enough, he will eventually fall and the side on which he will fall is predictable.

I'll admit my surprise when a golden-haired little lass suggested "G-A-M-E-S" as the next word. I thought I would get thirty-two "good answers," but she said a big "Bad!"

And when I asked her why, she said, "Cards."

"Cards?" I asked.

"Yes," she replied.

"What kind of cards?"

"Rook®!"

At the word Rook®, I began to wonder where I had been hiding out in the intervening years since college. I recalled the popularity of Rook® during academy and college (along with the near all-night sessions we had as we became absorbed in it)—but I hadn't heard of it for so long I guess I thought it had gone the way of marbles, tops, and "peg down."

Now it had surfaced and my memory also told me that it was after college-days that I learned that Rook® and a popular card game played in farm granges across the country were the same game—with different cards! The devil is a clever one. Rook® with its four suites in red, black, yellow, and green and the simple numbers 1–14 couldn't be dangerous!—not when played in Christian homes!

Isn't it amazing that the name of the game is Rook®—and rook means to cheat or defraud!

A man approached me at the close of a meeting one evening and told me a story that proved that a simple home game can have a "hook" in it.

"I was attending academy and I taught my roommate to play Rook®. He loved it. In fact, he couldn't get enough of it. Most of his time was spent learning how to shuffle and deal the cards. He became so expert that he discontinued his formal education and eventually became a professional gambler.

"Terror gripped my heart whenever I remembered that I was the one who started him down this road. I was afraid that he might lose his life—and I would be responsible for his soul.

"One time I learned that he was in Las Vegas working in a casino. I took time off from my job and flew to Vegas hoping I could get him to change his lifestyle.

"That evening when he was off duty, he came to my hotel and I was as glad to see him as he seemed to see me. After we discussed what had happened to our lives since school, I brought up the subject for which I had come. I pleaded with him to give up gambling, give his heart to the Lord—make a new start.

"You can only imagine my shock when he put his arm around my shoulders and said, 'Hey! Buddy! You taught me ... remember!' How I wished I could forget.

"The next day I made my way back to the airport with a heart still burdened with guilt. What more could I do?"

The story seemed ended. The man paused then said, "Last year my friend gave up gambling, gave his heart to Christ, and was baptized. Now I can rest easy. But you will never know the awful weight I carried on my conscience for over twenty years."

Consider these thought-provoking quotations:

Expertness in the *handling* of cards often leads to a desire to put this knowledge and tact to some use for personal benefit.... How many has this pernicious amusement led to every sinful practice, to poverty, to prison, to murder, and to the gallows! And yet many parents do not see the terrible gulf of ruin that is yawning for our youth. (MYP, p. 380)

...that which was considered harmless at home will not long be regarded as dangerous abroad. (MYP, p. 399)

Each person has his fringe, or grey, areas. The devil will see that he is well supplied, for many times Christians erect lion-defenses when the devil may be only a smart fisherman! "He does not always wear the ferocious look of the lion.... He can readily exchange the roar of the lion for the most persuasive arguments, or for the softest whisper." (2T, p. 287)

What then, is the guiding principle in those areas where neither the rules of right nor the rules of wrong seem to apply? The answer is found in the answer to a question. Do I want to live as close to God as I possibly can—or as close to the world? If the answer is toward God's side, then:

TO BE SAFE ONE MUST MOVE TO THE SIDE OF UNQUESTIONABLE RIGHT.

This takes one out of the fringe area, away from the balancing act on the tight rope, takes him out of the danger area. Only there will he be safe.

The devil is a sharp and persevering workman. He knows just how to entrap the unwary. But there is nothing he fears so much as that we shall become aware of and acquainted with his devices.

May God give us the perception to recognize these traps and the courage to move into the safe areas of God's side, for whatever else he may or may not be, the devil is a smart fisherman!

The Right

As a Christian, do you have to take abuse lying down or can you take it standing up?

One man said he didn't mind having people walk over him—if they didn't have spikes in their shoes! Too often Christians have the attitude that they must exhibit meekness and humility; they have no right to entertain or express their feelings.

This attitude can have some baleful results. A person who feels that he has no rights may "clam up" and lock his feelings inside. The result can be bitterness and depression. Or he can vigorously defend his rights—blow up—and end up with feelings of hatred and retaliation. Either way, the results are undesirable.

Does a Christian have rights? If so, how can he relate to abuse and still exhibit what is called the Christian attitude?

The morning mail brought a letter with an urgent appeal for help. A church in a distant city was having trouble with its new-church-building program—big trouble. At the moment, according to the writer, the work on the church was stopped. No money was coming into the building fund.

Of course, I knew that the work stoppage and lack of funds were not the *real* problems. They never are. I agreed to come.

After checking into a motel, I called the pastor, an intern just out of college. I could sense his frustration. He was fresh from school, eager, ambitious—and had landed in the middle of a problem. "What a way to enter the ministry," I thought.

I learned that there was a "split" in the church which could be spelled with a capital "S." It seemed that there were two influential members who had widely divergent views. The stronger of the two regarded the democratic process somewhat lightly as evidenced by the fact that when the church body voted one thing, he would, on his own, change it to his own preference.

About half of the church went along with him and his ideas (he was pretty convincing). The other half sided in with the other individual who felt that a majority vote should be followed. This caused the split. The disturbing thing was that the latter man became bitter over the whole thing and quit coming to church. Among the attending church members there was disunity; and animosity was deep and solid.

When the young pastor asked me what I was going to do, I said I didn't have the faintest idea except to pray. He said he was afraid, and I certainly concurred with this observation. So we prayed—prayed for wisdom—prayed for a solution.

The waiting was the hard part—it always is. The key to the solution, I felt, was the man who was not attending church, and the fact that he had a right to feel the way he did only compounded the problem. I freely admit that I was happy that Sabbath morning when the benediction ended the service for one could feel the tension over the whole congregation. It seemed to hang there like a pall.

That afternoon my wife and I drove out to the church site to look at the uncompleted structure. We found a beautiful building which needed only some finishing touches, lying there cold, empty. The feeling of disunity seemed to permeate even here.

We were about to leave when I heard women's voices and to my surprise the wife of the man who wasn't attending church came around a corner with some of her friends. After greetings were exchanged, she invited us to her house for an evening snack. I accepted immediately for I wanted to see her husband in some other situation than by a formal call. After all, what do you say to a man who has the right to feel the way he does?

On arriving at the house, my wife suggested that she help with the meal. My hostess led me to a comfortable chair in the living room. Going to a nearby hallway, she called, "Oh, Dear, Elder Rees is here."

She turned, smiled, and said, "Please make yourself comfortable; my husband will be out in a minute."

I waited. No "dear."

The ladies chatted in the kitchen and I sat.

After some time, my hostess peeked around the corner and saw me sitting there quite alone. She was embarrassed—apologized profusely—went to the hallway and gave the "dear call" again. Still no "dear."

It took three calls to produce results. When her husband came into the room, he didn't offer to shake hands, or even say, "Hi." He just blurted out, "Do you believe in the democratic process?" I assured him I did.

He sat on the arm of a divan and his pent-up feelings erupted in a torrent of words outlining everything that was wrong with the church in general and the building program in particular.

I really didn't listen too closely. I had heard it all before. Rather, I prayed, *Lord, what do I say to this man? How can I convince him he is wrong, when he is so right?*

Finally, the storm abated and I quietly said, "I am sure you are telling the truth for I have already heard the story."

He sat down beside me and asked, "What do you think we should do?"

(I answered the "we" part of the question.) "Why are you building a church?"

"We need more room."

"That isn't a good enough reason. Try another."

"We need more rooms for the lower divisions."

"Not good enough." He seemed puzzled, then a smile crept over his face as he groped for an answer that I might accept.

And finally, "So we can do soul-winning."

"I'll buy that." For isn't this the real purpose of the church? Soul winning? Certainly there are other reasons, important reasons such as a place to worship God, a haven for those who accept Christ, a school where we can learn of God's plans for us, but the church is really God's lighthouse in a benighted world.

"Can you do successful soul-winning without the agency of the Holy Spirit?" I asked.

"No," he admitted.

"Will the Holy Spirit work for and through the members of the church if there is disunity?"

"I guess not."

"Then, you had just as well sell the church (I knew there was another group wanting to buy it), for it won't accomplish what you have in mind."

He thought about this for a moment, then quietly asked, "What do you think 'I' should do?"

Quite frankly, I didn't know—but God did—and I heard myself saying, *"Sometimes we may have the right to feel the way we do but we dare not exercise this right if it will cause disunity.*" It was a foreign thought to me, but I felt a thrill for I knew this was God's answer to my friend's problem.

He didn't say whether he believed it or not, he really didn't have time to express an opinion for at that moment his wife called us to lunch. Over and over again during the meal I kept repeating silently this profound principle, "We may have the right, but...."

Following supper, we went to the church where a meeting had been called to discuss the church problems.

The pastor met me at the door and asked, "Would you do me a favor?"

"If I can," I replied.

"Will you please lead out in the meeting tonight—I'm scared."

"I'm scared too," I said, "but I'll do it."

We didn't have an opening song (who felt like singing?), but we had prayer, and the meeting began.

There was a lively discussion. I didn't say anything, only watched for any situation that might, in the heat of argument, get out of hand. A time or two it got a little "warm" but cooled quickly. After the entire program had been thoroughly reviewed, there was an awkward period of silence that had me puzzled. Just when I realized that I must say or do something this man (who had the right) stood up and, putting his hands on his hips, said, "All right! I've had my say! I think I have a perfect right to feel the way I do." He waited—then in a quiet, subdued tone, continued, "But I shouldn't have exercised that right, because it caused disunity and I'm asking each one of you to forgive me." He sat down.

The silence was leaden. No one moved. Then a man to my left got up, walked around me to this brother's side, put his hand on his shoulder and said, "You know, Brother, in the last few months I've said some awfully unkind things about you and I want you to forgive me."

I stepped back out of the way and watched as brother went to brother, arms went around shoulders and tears flowed freely. When God has an answer, it *really* works!

In case you are wondering, there *was* a problem but God had the answer, and that solved the problem.

One of the devil's most successful tactics is to bring in a spirit of disunity. Divide and conquer, is his plan. Harsh words, unjust acts are some of the things he uses to stir up bitter feelings to destroy harmony, for he knows that nothing can be accomplished in a climate of dissension and strife.

Someone asked why a Christian has to suffer mistreatment, slander, or abuse when he has renounced the world and dedicated his life to God.

"There is a high standard to which we are to attain if we would be children of God, noble, pure, holy, and undefiled; and a *pruning* process is necessary if we would reach this standard. How would this pruning be accomplished if there were no difficulties to meet, no obstacles to surmount, nothing to call out patience and endurance?" (5T, p. 344; Italics supplied).

A pruning process? I learned about this.

Some years ago we moved into the country and the first thing we did was to plant an orchard. In this orchard were three peach trees. The man who sold me the trees said that at the right time he would come and prune them.

They grew so beautifully. My wife and I were so proud of them. Now the time came when they should be pruned and I called the man. When he arrived and took his tools from the car, I began to wonder, for the trees weren't very large. When he began to cut and snip, I went into a state of shock! Almost. (My wife fled to the house under the pretext that she was going to start dinner.)

I finally asked meekly, "Do you have to cut so much off?"

"Do you want peaches?"

"Yes," I managed to gulp.

"Then you've got to prune them." I watched in silence. While he was washing for dinner, my wife whispered to me, "Is there anything left?"

"A few stumps and twigs," I said.

After he left, we went out to survey the disaster. My wife said, "Next year we won't call him."

I agreed.

He called us!

But ... we have had four crops of big, luscious peaches. He was right. If you want peaches, you have to be merciless with the pruning shears.

God wants Christians to bear fruit and He knows a pruning process is necessary. Notice this quotation:

> Life is disciplinary. While in the world, the Christian will meet with adverse influences. There will be provocations to test the temper; and it is by meeting these in the right spirit that the Christian graces are developed. If injuries and insults are meekly born, if insulting words are responded to by gentle answers, and oppressive acts by kindness, this is evidence that the spirit of Christ dwells in the heart. (5T, p. 344; Italics supplied).

The spirit of Christ is love and, according to I Corinthians 13, love has no limits. There is nothing it cannot face.

LOVE PLACES A PERSON IN A POSITION OF POSITIVE COMMAND.

Love allows the Christian to have feelings and emotions, but through its motivating force, he will choose not to exercise his rights if they might cause problems. Thus, he will be in a *position of positive command.* This is Christianity in action. Paul gave this formula when he wrote, "Be not *overcome* of evil, but *overcome* evil with good" (Rom. 12:21; Italics supplied).

There are two requisites for a positive Christian response in our social relations. First: *"Vengeance* is mine; I will repay, saith the Lord" (Rom. 12:19; Italics supplied). Second: "And be ye kind one to another, tenderhearted, *forgiving* one another, even *as God* for Christ's sake *hath forgiven you*" (Eph. 4:32; Italics supplied).

Then there are principles which can be applied which will bring peace and create harmony.

In the home the stress of day-to-day living can produce irritations but these can be greatly minimized if this principle is used.

"IF *PRIDE* AND *SELFISHNESS* WERE LAID ASIDE, FIVE MINUTES WOULD REMOVE MOST DIFFICULTIES" (EW, P. 119).

How well I remember watching two men as they applied this principle, and it took only thirty seconds to solve their differences!

A young wife once told me that when she tried to argue with her husband, he would always ask her, "would you rather be right—or nice?" Maybe this is what the father had in mind when he admonished his son, "Treat everybody with politeness even those who are rude to you. Remember that you show courtesy to others not because they are gentlemen, but *because you are one.*"

In the church, harmony is essential to its mission. It is the convincing evidence that God sent His Son to save sinners for we are told that nothing short of the miraculous power of God can take people with different backgrounds and dispositions and weld them into a unified body, their one aim being to exhibit the spirit and love of Jesus (9T, p. 194).

What principle applies when a decision has to be made and there are widely divergent views? (This relates to likes and dislikes, not matters of conscience.)

"They should also feel it a solemn duty to illustrate in their characters the teachings of Jesus, being at peace with one another and moving in perfect harmony as an undivided whole. *They should defer their individual judgment to the judgement of the body of the church*" (4T, p. 18; Italics supplied).

One of the most beautiful illustrations of the principle of Christian rights is found in the experience of Abraham with his nephew Lot. Abraham owned all the land on which they lived. Lot owed his uncle everything. He wouldn't have had anything if it hadn't been for Abraham. But, there was a problem. It seems the herdsmen of Abraham and the herdsmen of Lot were having problems over water holes, or grazing rights, and this came to the attention of Abraham.

He could have called Lot and told him that the land was his and that he had enough problems without these petty squabbles, that Lot should pack up his stuff and move into the mountains, leaving a buffer zone between their camps, but he didn't.

He took Lot to a point of land where they could look over the entire country and offered him *his* choice. Then he said, "Let there be no strife, I pray thee, between me and thee, and between my herdsmen and thy herdsmen; for *we be brethren*" (Gen. 13:8; Italics supplied). An unselfish spirit like Abraham's would solve all the difficulties we encounter with each other.

Paul gave a formula for dealing with those who mistreat us. "If thine enemy hunger, feed him; if he thirst, give him drink: for in so doing thou shalt heap coals of fire on his head" (Rom. 12:20).

I always thought this was pretty harsh treatment until I realized that when a person says or does something mean to another person, he automatically sets up within himself a guilty feeling. If he can get the other person to retaliate, *he transfers this guilty feeling to the other person.* If he is unable to transfer this guilt, he is forced to live with it and it is indeed "coals of fire on his head."

From fights, the Christian will simply walk away. For harsh words, he will give a soft answer. For arguments—silence. Douglas MacArthur said his grandfather once told him, "Don't say anything unless you can improve on silence." Silent influence will often do more than open controversy.

THIS IS THE VENGEANCE OF KINDNESS.

Once a person learns to control his emotions through the grace of Christ, although he may have the right to feel the way he does, he will *choose* not to exercise this right if it will create problems. Thus, he will find it much easier to adapt to any situation.

"...in the day of final accounts we shall see that all the obstacles we meet, all the hardships and annoyances that we are called to bear, are practical lessons in the application of principles of Christian life" (5T, p. 344).

When You Relax—Beware

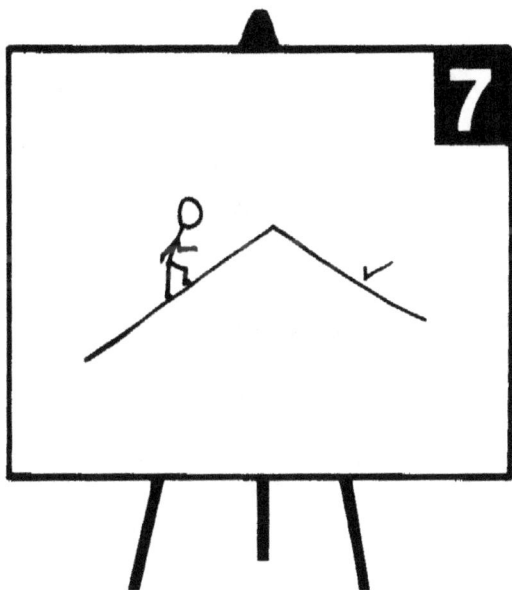

When you think you "have it made," and relax, you may be in trouble. Not that a person doesn't need periods of rest; both the body and mind require this, but these periods must be just that—a rest—never a letdown. It is well known that an athlete needs continual exercise to maintain muscle strength; the musician must constantly practice to stay in form. It is a law of nature that we either wear out or *rust* out. But rust comes from inactivity and is nonproductive, hence the danger.

My wife and I were camped near the Grand Tetons in Wyoming. These majestic mountains, many of which reach elevations higher than 10,000 feet above sea level, form a rugged backdrop for this land of lakes and rivers. But amidst this display of grandeur tragedy struck without warning on that day in June.

Two boys in their late teens climbed the Grand Teton (13,766 feet above sea level) which closely resembles the Matterhorn in Switzerland. They reached the top without incident and decided to take photographs to record their feat. The photographer couldn't get all of his partner in the view finder of the camera and asked him to step back a bit. That step was over 600 feet!

The almost sheer sides of the cliff presented a real challenge, but it was when they finally succeeded that they encountered their greatest danger.

This principle is found in the following quotation: "The season of inactivity that succeeds a great struggle is often fraught with greater danger than is the period of conflict" (PP, p. 555).

Israel's greatest dangers didn't come from their warlike enemies, but from their periods of ease and inactivity. They were warned by Moses before entering the promised land that economic success could lead to pride and self-confidence and there was real danger that they would forget their utter dependence upon God.

"Beware that thou forget not the Lord thy God...Lest when thou hast eaten and art full, and hast built goodly houses, and dwelt therein; And when thy herds and thy flocks multiply, and thy silver and thy gold is multiplied, and all that thou hast is multiplied; Then thine heart be lifted up, and thou forget the Lord thy God" (Deut. 8:11–14).

It is evident that they did forget, for the prophet Amos cried, "Woe to them that are ease in Zion" (Amos 6:1). History records the sad result of this forgetfulness.

Gideon, that mighty fighting man, could go into battle against the combined forces of the Midianites and Amalekites with only three hundred men because he followed God's instructions. But after this signal victory there was a period when there wasn't anything to do. He failed to wait for divine direction and began to plan for himself. This period of unrest proved to be a snare and he set up an unauthorized form of worship which led the people back into the idolatry which he had previously overthrown.

This principle of the danger in inactivity can be seen in the history of the nations of the world. They become strong through the intense struggle for power and leadership. But when they reach the point where this struggle is no longer necessary, they grow fat on their own commerce, lazy in their vision, and weak through luxury and idleness. At this point, they are vulnerable to adverse forces from within and without.

It isn't during the period of courtship that the marriage is in danger, but right after the marriage vows have been repeated. Then, instead of candlelit dinners in exotic little restaurants, there is a sink full of dirty dishes. Instead of sweet music bathing the senses, there is the jangling of the alarm clock, a reminder that there is work to be done—a family to support. Instead of infatuation, genuine love and respect must take over. This is the period of greatest danger.

A new convert often faces a period of intense conflict before he is brought into the fellowship of the church. He faces the loss of friends, relatives, sometimes his job. Then he gives his entire life to Christ and is baptized. That is when he faces the most difficult period in his experience.

Too often the members of the church appear to think, "Good, we got this one, let's go find another one" and forget that this new believer has critical needs. The church family must replace his lost friends, relatives and possibly assist him financially for a time. Often, this is not done and possibly this is why so many new converts enter the front door of the church only to go out the back.

The church itself is not immune to the danger of inactivity. Some years ago, I was working in a church that had passed through a real financial struggle building a house for God. The church was now completed and all the debts were paid. At this point, the members said they had worked so hard for so long that now they were going to *do something for themselves*.

They desperately needed a school where their children could get a Christ-centered education but they wouldn't consider this because *"It costs too much."* I tried in vain to point out the danger in not pushing ahead. I assured them that God would bless them in the future as He had blessed them thus far.

To my knowledge, this church has never made any significant progress. The younger, productive members have been forced to move to other localities for the education of their children, which left mostly old people in the church. These have neither the vigor nor the potential for an aggressive program.

In the Christian life there is an intense conflict, for the forces of good and the forces of evil are in deadly combat. The Christian dare not relax. He must always be vigilant and on the offensive *through the grace of God.*

"We must gain the victory over self, crucify the affections and lusts: and then begins the union of the soul with Christ.... After this union is formed, it can be preserved only by continual, earnest, painstaking effort" (5T. p. 47).

Paul admonished Timothy to "fight the good fight of faith" (I Tim. 6:12).

This principle of the danger in inactivity also applies to Christian benevolence. As we are constantly provided with the necessities of life, just so we are to be constantly giving of our time, influence, money—whatever is needed. There must be no lax periods, periods when we receive but do not give. Giving must be a principle that permeates the entire being.

If one gives from impulse or feeling, there will be periods when the emotions are not stirred. These are the danger points. Notice these danger points as indicated in the following diagram.

This kind of giving must be regarded as "unwise and dangerous."

A man once told me that he and his wife gave when and how they were impressed. From a conversation I accidently overheard, between the church treasurer and the pastor of his church, I concluded that these impressions were infrequent and not very strong. Jesus said, "Freely ye have received, freely give" (Matt. 10:8).

It is a law of the universe that one cannot stand still, he must either advance or retrograde. The Christian's progress must never be by spurts and jumps but by constant, earnest effort, ever forward and upward. Only in this way can he maintain his spiritual balance. The good steward may eventually wear out but he will never "rust" out.

I Work for God

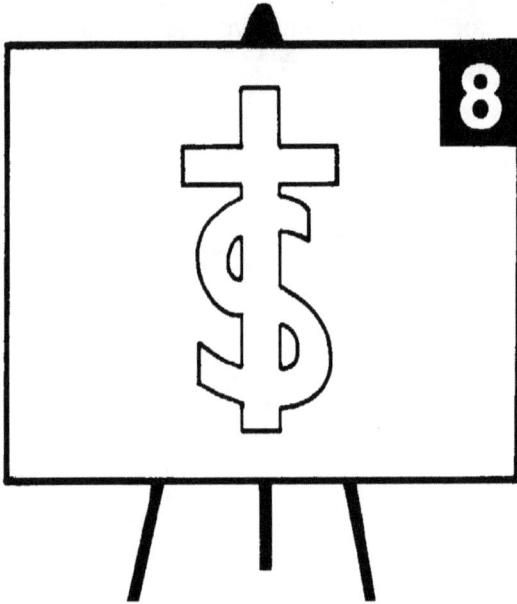

It is significant that Jesus Christ spent the majority of His life in the private sector, as a layman—a carpenter. This is really a shocking thought for most of us dwell with great interest on His public life and fail to consider the lessons available for us in those early years in Nazareth. However, we are told that He was doing God's service just as much during those years in His father's carpenter shop as when engaged in His public ministry.

Often, one reads or hears of someone who has decided to quit his job and go to work for the Lord. I remember visiting with a man one evening who had come to this decision. I tried to talk him out of it because I felt he was already working for God in a marked way. His position as an engineer took him to many countries of the world, where because of the nature of his work, he had many opportunities to witness to his faith.

At home, he was the main pillar of support for the little church to which he belonged. Because of this, it was possible to conduct a church school. He was active in giving Bible studies and there were members of the church as a result. I just couldn't believe that he wasn't exactly where God wanted him. Needless to say, I failed in my efforts to change his mind and I often wonder if he made the right decision. I don't know.

Possibly this unfortunate idea that there are some people who work for God and others who don't, stems back to some limited educational objectives. Being a doctor, preacher, or teacher was considered as a worthwhile goal while being a farmer, a merchant or a mechanic was regarded by some, at least, as only for those who were incapable of doing anything else.

For a girl, it was nurse, teacher, or secretary, but a housewife? Just a mother? And, still, in heaven's scales, "the mother who trains her children for Christ is as truly *working for God* as is the minister in the pulpit" (PK, p. 219; Italics supplied). A woman who realizes the importance of this role would never say, "I am *just* a housewife." (One wonders how she can properly train her children if she herself is uneducated!)

I am sure the devil wants us to separate our religious life from our business pursuits. He knows that if he is successful, he can nullify everything we profess. Ellen White wrote: "Religion and business are not two separate things, they are one. Bible religion is to be interwoven with all we do or say. Divine and human agencies are to combine in temporal as well as in spiritual achievements" (COL, p. 349).

Another of the devil's tricks is to spread the theory that work is degrading. This is a common fallacy in some third-world countries. Because of this, in some places, it is very difficult to provide work for unskilled students so they can earn their educational expenses. But is labor degrading?

God didn't think so. He placed our first parents in an orchard environment where they were to "dress and keep" it. Labor was to be a wonderful blessing, for in work man would find both fulfillment and contentment. In the growth and development of the products of the field he could better understand the designs of his Creator. Labor was to be an educator.

After sin entered the world, man was told, "In the sweat of thy face shalt thou eat bread" (Gen. 3:19). From this some folks think that labor was part of the curse. On the contrary, labor has proved to be man's greatest blessing. "The sleep of the labouring man is sweet, whether he eat little or much: but the abundance of the rich will not suffer him to sleep" (Eccles. 5:12).

The proof of this observation can be seen in the boredom and unhappiness of the so-called "jet set" who maintain villas in many places and fly from one to the other, never satisfied. In one area where all the people belong to this class, it is reported that there are more psychiatrists per capita than in any other place in the world. What they really need is the satisfaction of some productive work.

Work is a great character developer. Children are to be taught that anything that needs to be done is honorable. Work is never to be considered as desirable or undesirable but rather as essential or nonessential. Attention to detail, thoroughness, dispatch and decisions are contributing factors to character development. "Whatsoever thy hand findeth to do, do it with thy might," is the advice of the wise man (Eccles. 9:10).

But how about working for God? Is this just a specialty? Limited to a few people? Is only a particular kind of labor considered working for God?

We have been instructed that we can worship God just a thoroughly while we are erecting a building as we can in a religious service. But how many carpenters, as they are hammering and sawing, consider that they are working for God. However, Christian businessmen can weave the great principles of truth into their everyday transactions.

Not only do those who labor in the world's commerce or have businesses in the world's marts have the opportunity to further the gospel through their means, but they have a greater opportunity to witness through their influence. Some of the outstanding men of the Bible either did not come from a ministerial background, or did not become preachers. Elisha was a farmer on the hills of Gilboa when God called him from his plow to lead Israel into a great reformation.

Joseph was the favorite son of a doting father when he was thrust into the harsh life of a slave. He was a good slave—so good, in fact, that ere long he was put in charge of all his master's possessions. Because of his recognition of the restriction in stewardship, and his moral integrity, he was thrown into prison where he languished for over two years. But he was a good prisoner and from prison he was made prime minister of Egypt (and master over his former owner!). During all this time, can anyone say he wasn't working for God?

Nehemiah was a waiter in the kings court when he was chosen to superintend the rebuilding of the walls of Jerusalem.

But for sheer courage and audacity who can match the little girl who was snatched from her Judean home, carried off to Damascus and given to a captain's wife as a slave. She could have been filled with hatred for the man who had treated her so cruelly but she wasn't. One day as she watched her master, she shyly said to her mistress, "I wish…I wish that my master was with the prophet in Samaria for he would heal him of his leprosy." She had pity for this Syrian and Syrians were notorious for their lack of pity.

The mistress told the master and he told the king and he called the state department. In no time at all, Naaman, with an honor guard, safe conduct pass, $6,000 in silver, $55,000 in gold, and ten very expensive suits, thundered out of the gates of Damascus heading for Samaria and healing.

A knowledge of the true God was brought to an entire nation. How long would it have taken an evangelistic team to do what she did? Although she was only a slave, she was working for God.

Sometimes we get the idea that Jesus was advising everyone to leave their jobs and go to work for Him because He called Peter, James and John from the fish business, and Matthew from the internal revenue service. But He didn't ask His best friend Lazarus to do this, or Zacchaeus or Nicodemus ... or even that crazy fellow who rushed out of the tombs threatening Jesus and the disciples as they beached their boats in the country of the Gadarenes.

He really wanted to go to work for the Lord. After the demons left him for the bunch of swine, he was sitting clothed and in his right mind, and he asked Jesus, "Please let me go with you."

But Jesus said, "Go home to thy friends, and tell them how great things the Lord hath done for thee" (Mark 5:19). Possibly this is the key to working for God, the personal witness.

It was camp-meeting time, the service was over, but I stopped to talk so it was late and the cafeteria was crowded. I put my food on a tray and was looking around for some place to put it when I saw a hand in the far corner of the room and a finger beckoning me. A man, his wife and little boy were seated at the table. There was an extra chair. "Come, join us," he invited.

After thanking God for the food, I asked them their names. Then I asked about his work.

"I work for a large corporation as an engineer."

"Have you been an Adventist long?"

"No. Only two years."

"How did you become an Adventist?"

"Well, that's a long story." He turned and glanced at his wife.

Some message passed between them which whetted my curiosity, so I said, "Well, I have two and a half hours before my next meeting." (I noticed some people in the surrounding area also showed interest and I soon learned why, for it was a fantastic story.)

He grew up in a home where he had never seen a Bible. His father was an atheist, his mother didn't believe in anything. He had never been to Sunday School a day in his life and had nothing to do with religion. He didn't believe there was a God. Life was simply here and now, and that was the end of it. But he had goals. A good education, a good job, a home and family—in that order. He got his degree in engineering and landed a position with this major corporation. Everything was on schedule.

In the department where he worked, there was a Christian engineer—a witnessing Christian.

"Boy, how he witnessed," he said. "He was always giving me literature or books, inviting me to some meetings, wanting me to listen to some radio program or watch some TV broadcast. The literature and books I threw away. I never had time to listen to the radio or TV. But he kept after me.

"Finally, it began to bug me and one day I went into his office and said, 'Look, you're a nice guy. I like you—but let's leave this religion bit alone. Okay? I don't believe there is a God and, anyway, I'm not interested.'

"And he said, 'Okay,' and never mentioned it again.

"But, he went on to say, "there was something about this fellow that attracted me. He was always so calm. I remember one time when he was being blamed for something I knew he wasn't responsible for and he never said anything. Finally, I stormed into his office and asked him why he didn't tell a few people off. After all, I reminded him, 'It isn't your fault.' You know what he did?

"He just smiled and said, 'I know, but now everybody's upset. It'll be all right.' I didn't get it.

"But what bothered me most was that on days I had planned to go fishing, or play golf, I would find myself over at his house, following him around, helping. I couldn't seem to stay away."

He said he bought a house and furniture and went back to his home state where he married his girlfriend. Sometime later a little boy came along to complete his dream. Now everything was turning up roses.

Then one morning—one Sunday morning—they were having breakfast and he said he had some egg on the fork halfway from the plate to his mouth, when his wife said, "My son and I are going to join a church."

He carefully put the egg back on the plate and said very calmly, "Let's get something straight. There's not going to be any religion in this house."

She set her jaw, and replied, "You can stay home, but I'm not going to have my son grow up outside the church."

Holding up his hands, he said, "Hold it! Hold it! Wait a minute, back up. What this family does, it's going to do together. Get your coat."

"My coat?"

"Yeah, get your coat. Don't argue with me, just get your coat."

He picked up the little boy and got his coat. When they were in the car, his wife asked, "Where are we going?" He didn't say anything, just drove.

Pulling up in front of his friend's house, they got out, rang the doorbell, and his friend opened the door with a big smile and said, "Come in. Come on in. My, but it's good to see you."

"I asked him, 'What church do you go to?'

"'Why, I'm a Seventh-day Adventist.'

Then, turning to his wife, he said, "That's where we're going."

"I never heard of it," she replied.

"Neither did I—but that's where we're going."

Turning to his friend, he asked, "What are you supposed to do?"

Surprised, his friend answered, "Well, I suppose you should have some Bible studies."

"Well, here we are. Let's get started."

And that is how this engineer became a Seventh-day Adventist.

"How do you feel about it now?" I wondered.

"Greatest two years in my life," was his reply.

"Mine, too," added his wife.

Then, after a moment he said, "You have no idea how happy I am that my friend *lived his religion.*"

Neither our greatest evangelist, nor our finest author would have had any influence on this man, because he just wasn't interested. It took the personal witness of a man who was *working for God.*

In God's original plan, possibly man wouldn't have needed so many different talents. After he sinned, the first thing he needed was a tailor—then some gardening tools, medical attention and, later, an undertaker. God has always given us the talents we need and each of them is useful and essential. And one cannot say that one is more important than any other.

Weaving religious principles into the business life was paramount in the time of Israel. There were farmers, artisans, physicians and those who cared for the temple. By their health and prosperity, they would be an object lesson to the world, that they worshiped the true God.

Their business practices were to be an integral part of this witness. They were instructed, "You shall not pervert justice in the measurement of length and weight or quantity. You shall have true scales and true weights, true measures, dry and liquid" (Lev. 19:35, 36, NEB). What a mighty witness this would have been in a world filled with chiselers and cheaters. How much we need these principles in the world of commerce today!

It is true that sometimes God calls men from their business pursuits to do a special work for Him, but we are warned against leaving our present position unless the Lord clearly indicates. Our lot may be difficult, but often the Lord places us in these circumstances for a definite reason.

The active man in business, as he is brought into contact with the world will have trials and perplexities. He will find there is a tendency to let worldly thoughts and plans crowd into his devotional life. But he has the promise that divine grace awaits his demand.

HIS GREAT NEED WILL BE THE MIGHTY ARGUMENT WHICH WILL PREVAIL WITH GOD.

The active man of business will always remember that he is a steward of the living God. He will handle the things under his control as if the Owner were managing them Himself. He is solely responsible for an honest day's labor, and for Christian business practices, for he is always working for God.

Accidents and/or Mistakes

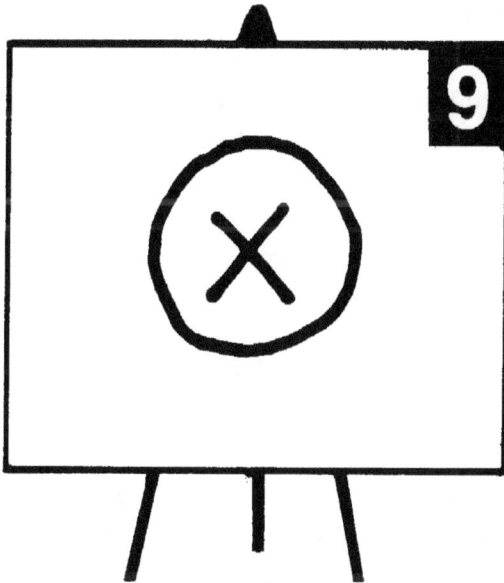

My friend sat behind the wheel of his car trying to figure out what he was going to do next. That is, he was sitting in what was left after the guardrails on either side of the road had removed most of the front as well as the rear of his car.

He doesn't recall exactly what happened—maybe it was loose gravel—maybe he went to sleep—at any rate, here he was crosswise of the highway.

A lady following him saw his car go out of control and bounce from rail to rail, flipping sundry bits of automobile into the air. She skidded to a stop, rushed up beside his car and said, "Are you hurt?"

"No," he calmly replied.

"Are you sure you aren't hurt...do you need a cup of coffee?"

"No, lady, I'm not hurt, and I don't need a cup of coffee. Why should I?"

"Why—th-th-th-the accident!"

"Oh, lady! That happened a minute ago."

"But—how can you be so calm...why-why-why I'd be so upset I'd be climbing the walls."

"Lady," he said, "you can't do anything about something that's happened, even if it was only a second ago, so never waste your time worrying about that. I'm sitting here trying to decide if I should go to this next town and buy a car to haul all this stuff home—or if I should ship it and take the bus."

Somehow my friend has learned to control his emotions in unfortunate happenings so he doesn't waste time fretting about them and thus make wrong decisions which result in inappropriate actions. This is a rare accomplishment for most people react to accidents and mistakes in an irresponsible manner, and end up often regretting their hasty actions.

How many times does a person say, at a later date, "If I could have thought clearly at the time, I would have done things differently." Why didn't he think clearly? The answer is that the emotions and feelings were in control, and these are very unstable motivators. Calm decisions and actions are rarely made under stress. How, then, can one deal with stressful situations?

First, one must remember, as my friend said, that it is impossible to do anything about something that has happened even if it was only a second ago. No act, no word can ever be retrieved. They are forever embossed in history as if engraved in stone. Therefore, one must learn to cope with circumstances *which cannot be altered.*

This is of special significance to the Christian for it is one of the devil's traps to involve him in situations that will produce adverse feelings and reactions, then fill his mind with regrets and guilt. If Satan can get the Christian in the habit of always regretting something that has happened over which he has no control, then he will transfer this to his spiritual life and *he won't believe that his sins are forgiven.*

This unbelief in the atoning blood of Christ will result in despair and bitterness and the person will face a hopeless future constantly harassed by the specter of his past mistakes.

But how can a person control his feelings? Are there corrective steps that can lead one to the place where he can think clearly and act wisely under all circumstances?

In a sin-cursed, accident-prone world there are bound to be unfortunate incidents, some of them disastrous. But in these happenings, disturbing though they be, the Christian can condition himself for spiritual stability and maturity.

There are three basic steps which will aid in this conditioning process.

In the Material Life

(1) *Adapt or readjust.* If one has a car accident and the car is no longer operable, obviously some other arrangements for transportation are going to have to be made.

If the main dish on the menu lands in the middle of the kitchen floor, some substitute is called for. In either case, one must concentrate on the adjustment, not on the accident.

(2) *Take steps to correct.* If the car accident was caused by hurry, fatigue or emotional stress—another accident may be avoided by recognizing and correcting the causative agent.

If one steps on a skate lying at the bottom of the stairs and takes off like one of the flying Wallendas, teach the children to put their toys away. (The bones won't stand too much of this sort of thing.) Take corrective steps.

(3) *Forget it.* You can't do anything about what has happened except to adjust or correct, so forget it. Isn't it amazing how people will talk and laugh about some quite serious incident some years after the event? Time has a calming effect. By

proper procedures and attitudes this calming effect can be accelerated.

In the Spiritual Life

(1) *Learn something from it.* Mistakes and sins can be either stumbling blocks or learning steps. Speaking of her youth, one lady said that she remembers doing things which were wrong, some worse than others, and each time she expected her father to scold her, but he never did. All he would say was, "Did you learn anything from this experience?" He was wise enough to recognize that even unfortunate experiences are valuable only if we learn something from them.

(2) *Ask God for forgiveness and believe that you are forgiven.* Every Christian has this promise, "If we confess our sins, he is faithful and just to forgive us our sins, and to cleanse us from all unrighteousness" (I John 1:9).

(3) *Forget it.* If God has promised to separate us from our sins as far as the "east is from the west," to put them in the "bottom of the sea," to change them from scarlet to "whiter than snow," it is certain He doesn't want us to wear them around our necks like a yoke, constantly remembering, constantly regretting. Remember, you can't do anything about what has happened, so forget it.

This is the same principle the Apostle Paul gave to the Philippians. *"Forgetting those things which are behind,* and reaching forth unto those things which are before, I press toward the prize of the high calling of God in Christ Jesus" (Phil. 3:13, 14; Italics supplied).

He knew that a person running a race can't be constantly looking back and hope to win. The same principle applies to the Christian's race.

I will always be indebted to the lady who was kind enough to copy the following quotation in my notebook while I was talking with some people at the close of a meeting. Unfortunately, I did not get her name before she mingled with the departing members.

"There are two days in every week about which we should not worry, two days which should be kept free from fear and apprehension.

"One of these days is yesterday with its mistakes and cares—its faults and blunders—its aches and pains. All the worry in the world cannot bring back yesterday—we cannot erase a single word we said—yesterday is gone!

"The other day is tomorrow with its possible adversities—its burdens—its large promise and poor performance. Tomorrow's sun will rise either in splendor or behind a mask of clouds—but it will rise. Until it does, we have no stake in it—for it is yet unborn. This leaves only one day—today!

"Any man can fight the battle of just one day—it is only when you and I add the burden of those two awful eternities—yesterday and tomorrow—that we break down. It is not the experience of today that drives men mad—it is remorse or bitterness for something which happened yesterday and the dread of what tomorrow may bring.

"Let us therefore live but one day at a time!" (Anonymous)

Would it not be worthwhile to make a pledge like this: With God's help, I will try to forget the happenings of the day that is past, *whether good or bad*, and greet each new day as the best in my life.

If we remember the bad things which happened yesterday, this will tarnish the beautiful things of today. If we remember how good yesterday was, it will make the unfortunate events of today seem darker.

"Let the fresh blessings of *each new day* awaken praise in our hearts for these tokens of His loving care. When you open your eyes in the morning, thank God that He has kept you through the night. Thank Him for His peace in your heart. Morning, noon, and night, let gratitude as a sweet perfume ascend to heaven" (MH, p. 253; Italics supplied).

Always remember that you can't do anything to change an unfortunate happening *even if it was only a second ago*, so don't waste time in regretting it. Energy spent in regretting is wasted energy. Energy must be used in future planning and action. This is the key to positive Christian living.

Listening

Most people know how to talk but few know how to listen.

The reason is that we often confuse hearing with listening. Hearing is receiving sound, but listening requires some response: thought, an answer or some type of action.

When a child either disobeys or fails to carry out his mother's directions, one often hears the mother say, "Did you hear me?" And the child answers, "I heard you." Then the mother says, "But *you aren't listening.*" The child heard sounds all right but there was no response.

A great deal of emphasis is placed on effective speaking and writing but little has been done in the way of teaching people to listen. The result is an enormous loss of time, energy and money.

A survey of a large company revealed the alarming fact that the listening efficiency of the employees was less than fifty percent! This meant that less than half of what was being said was being understood in some constructive way.

In another plant where a serious quality control was costing large sums of money, the solution to the problem came to light when a valued employee tendered his resignation. When asked by the personnel manager for a reason, he said he was tired of being treated like a dumbbell! He further stated that he had known what the problem was from the beginning.

"Why didn't you say something?" he was asked.

"I tried," he replied, "but nobody would listen. The foreman wouldn't listen—the plant manager wouldn't listen…I'm quitting!"

It is almost a cliché in marital disputes that there is a lack of communication. It is certainly not from a shortage of words, but nobody seems to be listening.

Possibly one reason why people don't listen is because listening is hard work, it takes real concentration. Sound comes to us through a thick screen of distractions, both physical and psychological. External sounds often must compete with internal factors for attention. Consider some of the tricks the mind often plays on us.

It may dart ahead and either anticipate or jump to a conclusion. Sometimes the hearer simply lacks interest in what is being said (may possibly be bored by it) for the mind tends to hear what it wants to hear. (Praise is always more acceptable than criticism). The most common problem is that the mind concentrates on the answer rather than on what is being said. This creates a major roadblock in communication.

At least some of these are caused by certain characteristics of the mind. It has been determined that the average person speaks at the rate of about one hundred twenty-five words per minute—

but the mind operates at about *five hundred words per minute!* This ratio of one hundred twenty-five to five hundred makes it easy to understand why the mind tends to dart ahead unless it is kept under strict control.

Another study in communications shows that of the five hundred most commonly used words there can be *fourteen thousand separate meanings!* What we imagine or think a person means may not be what he has in mind at all. This points up the difficulty in trying to keep pace with the listener's mind and being sure he gets the *right* message.

Listening was one of the problems in the ministry of Jesus. Many heard Him but few listened. "The world's Redeemer had many hearers, but few followers" (7T, p. 36).

Mark 8 records a miracle of the feeding of the four thousand. In this instance, there were only seven loaves and a few fish, but they took up seven baskets of fragments. Following this, Jesus and His disciples crossed the lake to Dalmanutha. Waiting for them to land were some Pharisees who wanted to get into some theological discussion and asked for a sign. Jesus said no sign would be given them. He returned to the boat and directed His disciples to go back across the lake.

As they were riding along, He said, "Beware of the leaven of the Pharisees."

One disciple said to another, "Do you know why He said that?"

He answered, "No."

Then he told him, "It was because *we forgot to bring the lunch!*"

They heard what Jesus said but they didn't understand what he meant. They were hearing but not listening.

Referring to a former miracle when He fed the five thousand, Jesus asked how many baskets of fragments were picked up and they answered, twelve. Then He asked how many baskets remained after the feeding of the four thousand. They answered, seven. Then He said, "Having eyes, see ye not; and having ears, *hear ye not?*"

When He gave the parable of the sower, he cautioned, "Take heed therefore *how ye hear.*" It wasn't *what* they heard that was as important as *how.*

In the Bible "to hear" is often used for listening to the word of God with the firm purpose of obeying. When God "hears" our prayers, it is in the sense of answering them. When God spoke to the youthful Samuel, he replied, "Speak; for thy servant *heareth*" (I Sam. 3:10; Italics supplied). He was saying that what God told him to do, he would do.

When the Philistines invaded Israel one time and defeat appeared imminent, the people asked Samuel to appeal to God in their behalf. "And Samuel cried unto the Lord for Israel; and the Lord *heard him.*" God answered his prayer with lightning, thunder and hailstones, defeating the enemy.

Because the eyes and ears are the chief avenues to the soul, the devil places cleverly designed traps to catch even the most cautious. Consider some of his devices.

Trap 1. We listen to the wrong things.

To be safe, one must avoid reading, seeing or hearing those things which could prove detrimental to spiritual life. The mind must not be left to dwell on evil or impure thoughts suggested by the enemy. Even as innocuous as a newspaper seems to be, it is not without danger. "It seems as if the enemy is at the foundation of the publishing of many things that appear in the newspapers" (AH, p. 404).

Trap 2. We do not want to listen.

"Then drew near unto him all the publicans and sinners for to hear him. And the Pharisees and scribes murmured, saying, 'This man receiveth sinners, and eateth with them'" (Luke 15: 1, 2).

This attitude of the scribes and Pharisees is similar to that of those who don't want to hear because it might conflict with their life style or personal ideas. They feel that if they don't hear they won't be held accountable. (Anyone who thinks this should plead ignorance the next time he is stopped by a traffic officer and see if this is a valid excuse.)

Trap 3. We don't take time to listen.

I wonder what we would think if some friend came to visit and from the time he arrived until he left never gave us a chance to say anything. And, yet, we talk to God (supposedly as to a friend) but when do we give Him time to answer? It is usually, "Bless this and that and, thank you, Lord, for everything, Amen," but do we ever listen for a reply?

It was in a series of meetings in Martinique that I observed four young ladies as they came to the church each evening. They would kneel just inside the door to pray, then make their way to seats near the front of the auditorium. Here they would kneel to pray again. After they took their seats, they would sit quietly with bowed heads, and now they were ready for the service. They took time to listen.

There seems to be a pattern today that everything has to be *fast and loud*...that silence is to be avoided at any cost, that silence is an evidence of some breakdown in the program. Wouldn't it be wonderful if somewhere, somehow a place and time could be set apart for just listening, listening to what God has to say to us? God spoke to Elijah in a "still, small voice" but in many places today it would be difficult to hear *any* voice.

Trap 4. We listen for other people.

Jesus referred to this trap. "And why beholdest thou the mote that is in thy brother's eye, but perceivest not the beam that is in thine own eye?" (Luke 6:410. One never truly *listens* when applying what is being said to someone else.

Trap 5. We listen to men rather than to God.

I remember so vividly the evening when a man asked me what I thought he should give to a particular church program. Because I hadn't completed my surveys and set up suggested family goals by this time, I could frankly tell him that I hadn't the faintest idea.

"But I thought you were an expert," was his reply.

"Not really," I said, "but I know two people who *know* what you ought to do."

"Oh...who are they?"

"Well, you are the one and God is the other."

"You really mean that?" he said.

"Of course, I do. If I were going to give some of my Partner's money away, I would certainly ask Him about it first."

He smiled, thanked me and left. A couple of nights later just before another meeting, the same man asked, "Are we going to sign something—or something?"

"Yes, something," I answered.

"Could I see it?"

"Certainly, I replied, and went to my supplies and brought back a pledge card. He took it and found a seat on the other side of the room.

I was busy studying some notes on the lectern when I saw this pledge card placed right on top of them. I looked at it carefully. (How could I help it, it covered my notes.) It was completely filled out with name, address, telephone number ... and the *amount!* I couldn't believe my eyes.

You see, I had completed my surveys by this time and had set a suggested goal for this man in my mind, but the amount he had chosen was at least two times what I had in mind.

"That must have been some conversation," was my comment.

"It was," he said. "When I got home the other night, I got down on my knees and asked, 'Lord, have I been selfish?' and He said, 'You surely have been.'"

(I don't' know how God communicated to him, I didn't think it would be appropriate to ask.) He was thoughtful for a moment, then continued, "You know, I love the Lord, I don't want to be selfish and I'm going to do something about it."

I cringe when I think that I might have "jammed" God's communication system by making a suggestion which would have been far below what He had in mind. While God does speak to men through other men, one must be very careful to keep tuned to God's "channel" for it's on a different frequency.

Trap 6. We tune out God's voice.

It was a week of prayer at an academy. One of my duties was to counsel students who had problems they wished to discuss. One day a boy asked for an interview with the suggestion that we go some place where we wouldn't be disturbed. He located an unoccupied room. I found a seat as he closed the door. He sat down and appeared to be searching for words to begin, then asked cautiously, "Do you think it's all right for me to kiss my girlfriend?"

Slightly off balance, I said, "How would I know if it's all right for you to kiss your girlfriend or not? Why, is there some rule against it?"

"Yes."

"What happens if you get caught?"

"They put us on social."

"What's social?" And he explained that certain privileges were taken away.

"Are there some kids who have been caught and are on social?"

"Sure."

"How come you were never caught?"

"Well, you see, I'm in charge of the science lab. My girl takes chemistry, so we get back behind the shelves."

I thought about this. He waited.

Finally, "I don't think I'd worry about whether it was right or wrong to kiss your girlfriend."

"You don't?" His face brightened.

"No, I don't think so. I think I would worry about something else."

"What's that?"

"Well, you must have a very sensitive conscience. It must be so sensitive that in little things like kissing girlfriends, it says, 'Hold it. Wait a minute, you shouldn't do that, you know.' And if you say to your conscience, 'I really appreciate your concern, but this is *no big deal*, this is nothing,' your conscience will think you don't want to be reminded of 'little' things—like kissing girlfriends.

"Then you may do something a little more serious and your conscience will say, 'Hey man, wait a minute, you'd better not do that.' And you reply, 'Thank you, you know, I really appreciate your looking after me, but this is no big deal.' And your conscience will block out another level of 'little' things you don't want to be warned about.

"If you continue to say 'no' to your conscience long enough, the time could come when you would walk into a service station, pull out a gun, and say, 'Reach for the sky—this is a stickup!' The attendant might make a sudden move and you could stand there pumping bullets into his body as he slumps to the floor."

He covered his face with his hands and said in a choked voice, "I could *never* do that."

"Oh, yes, you could, for that's how a man gets to this point, by saying 'no' to his conscience one time too many."

He thought about this for awhile, then asked, "What if my girlfriend doesn't want to stop?"

"Now, I really have advice for you," I replied. "If you have a girlfriend who doesn't want you to follow your conscience, I would suggest you start running—and run—and run—and keep on running, for if you ever marry her, you will really know what hell on earth is all about and you won't have to wait long to find out."

We had prayer, he thanked me, and left. The next day I was walking down the hallway when a hand reached out and pulled me into the alcove of a doorway. It was my young friend.

"I told her," he whispered.

"What did she say?"

"She said she was glad because she didn't feel right about it, either."

"You know something?"

"What?"

"I think you have a real nice girlfriend."

He smiled a happy smile.

God talks to us through the still, small voice of conscience. How careful we must be to *listen*—for if we say "no" then we set up a pattern, and each no response will make it more difficult to hear God's voice—until, finally, we won't hear it at all.

A Christian may have excellent hearing but to *listen* to God's voice he must be spiritually awake.

Responsibility

What responsibility, if any, does the man on the road have to the man in the ditch?

Three goose hunters were hiding in a blind about a quarter mile from a game refuge. It was a warm day, clear and sunny— "bluebird weather" —and the birds were flying in and out of the refuge too high for their guns. As they sat there talking, reluctant to go home, they heard the "goose talk" of a flight returning to the refuge from their feeding grounds.

This flock seemed much lower and although they were still very high, one man (shooting a magnum) decided to try to reach them. He shot three times and heard the shot rattle against their wings. His partners laughed about this waste of ammunition until they saw one goose leave the formation, set her wings and start gliding toward the ground.

Realizing that she would land close to the refuge fence, the hunter left his gun behind and raced after her—but stopped suddenly—not believing what he was seeing. A large gander left the flock, dove under his wounded mate, and carried her on his back to safety!

Some instinct in that so-called unintelligent bird caused him to assist his mate to safety. Contrast this incident with that found in Genesis 4:9 "And the Lord said unto Cain, Where is Abel, thy brother? And he said, I know not: Am I my brother's keeper?"

When Cain was asked about his brother, why didn't he say, "I don't know," and go on weeding his onions? Why did he say, "Am I my brother's keeper?" The spirit of Cain is the spirit of the world. This lack of concern for others is the basis for all the hatred and strife that plague mankind.

Strangely enough, the Christian community is not exempt from this same malady, for in no other area is the average Christian so derelict as in the area of responsibility. In some instances, this may be due to lack of understanding of what constitutes responsibility but probably the real reason is good, old-fashioned selfishness.

Pure religion *is* responsibility. "Is this not the fast I have chosen? to loose the bands of wickedness, to undo the heavy burdens, and let the oppressed go free, and that ye break every yoke. Is it not to deal *thy* bread to the hungry, and that *thou* bring the poor that are cast out to *thy* house? When *thou* seest the naked, that *thou* cover him" (Isa. 58:6, 7; Italics supplied).

This text certainly doesn't picture the Christian as a *referral* service—directing the unfortunate to the church, or local welfare agency. It places the responsibility squarely on him. The words "thy" and "thou" bring this great principle to its focal point— individual responsibility.

James separates pure religion from a formal profession. "Pure religion and undefiled before God and the Father is this, To visit the fatherless and widows in their affliction, and to keep himself unspotted from the world" (James 1:27).

It would appear that Job clearly understood this for although he was the richest man in the East and must have delegated a great deal of authority—*he ran his own welfare service!* "I was eyes to the blind, and feet was I to the lame. I was father to the poor: and the cause which I knew not *I searched out*" (Job 29:15, 16; Italics supplied). Job didn't wait to be solicited for aid—he went looking for opportunities.

Jesus told the story of a traveler who was held up by some bandits on the Jericho road. These thugs not only robbed him but also beat him so badly he was left half dead in the ditch.

A preacher came by, but he was late for an appointment, and he was wearing his best black suit, so he didn't stop. A local elder appeared next, but things looked kind of messy ... and besides the robbers might just be waiting in the bushes. He didn't even alert the Highway Patrol!

But a salesman, who really didn't make any profession, stopped, gave what assistance he could, and took the poor fellow to the nearest motel. He cared for him all night and in the morning not only paid for his night's lodging but also promised to cover any additional expenses when he made his next trip.

This story has to be more than first-aid by the roadside. It strikes at the very heart of personal responsibility. What is my obligation to my fellow man? What if this obligation requires personal risk, what then?

A safe rule might be that we render assistance *commensurate with the circumstances*. This might call for personal assistance and involvement. There are other times when the nature of the situation might indicate that the proper authorities be notified. In either case, we dare not simply ignore the plight of our fellow men and "pass by on the other side of the road." We are personally responsible to see that the situation is cared for in some way.

Consider these areas of responsibility.

Our responsibility to God.

"And God said, Let us make man in our image…and let them have dominion…" (Gen. 1:26). Dominion is responsibility. Whether we use such terms as superintendent, foreman, or manager, the relationship to the owner is the same, i.e., responsibility for the things under our control and accountability for them.

Adam was responsible for the "fish … fowl … cattle … and all the earth." The creation of Eve increased his responsibility as did every subsequent increase.

We are responsible for the time, talents and influence which have been entrusted to us, as well as the material goods in our possession. We are also responsible for our neighbor and must treat him as we would wish to be treated.

Our responsibility to the individual.

Two friends have planned a pack trip in the mountains. Extensive preparations have been made. On the appointed day they drive to the end of the road, don their packs and set off up the trail. They have gone perhaps three miles when one of them falls from the trail and is injured.

Can the other simply say, "My, that's tough luck, but sometimes that's how the ball bounces … but there's no use spoiling my trip" and take off up the trail? Social acceptance demands that he render whatever assistance is required—*even if it means canceling the entire trip!*

But, what if the two hikers come upon a total stranger who is injured. What then? The same rule applies—yes, *even if it means canceling the entire trip!*

This responsibility may extend far beyond the point of personal contact or even time.

A friend and I were taking a trip in a mountainous area for the first time. We had been directed to cross a bridge over a river and climb a steep hill on the other side at the top of which we would find a signpost which would indicate the right road.

We found the signpost and took the road indicated but it went downhill. We wondered about this, for it seemed we should be following a ridge, not head back toward the river. We really began to wonder when we came to a rickety bridge spanning a deep ravine.

My friend stopped the car. I walked out on the bridge and jumped up and down a few times. (I'm not sure at this point exactly what that proved.) It seemed safe, so he inched the car across. (I walked.) The old bridge swayed and groaned, but he made it. About a hundred yards farther on, we came to the end of the road—and an abandoned mine!

We had to cross that bridge again. When we arrived at the fork in the road, we looked at the signpost carefully and found that someone had "playfully" turned it around.

On our return trip, three days later, a sign blocked the road to the mine with the warning "BRIDGE OUT." We hiked down to see and, sure enough, the old rickety bridge was in the bottom of the canyon. I guess our two crossings were too much for its aging timbers.

If that bridge had collapsed when we crossed it, whoever turned that sign around would have been just as responsible for our deaths as if they had personally taken our lives.

Group responsibility.

When a person joins a group, his responsibility increases by the number of persons in the group and to the group as a body. Likewise, each member now has an additional responsibility and the group as a whole is responsible to him.

Certain group responsibilities are basic to the welfare of any community. For mutual benefit, we have educational systems, police and fire departments, assistance for the aged and the unemployed. As a resident of a state, we have individual and collective responsibilities. Each citizen has obligations and responsibilities to his country.

A person automatically assumes certain responsibilities when he becomes a member of the church. But it is a sobering fact that in the average church about one-third of the members carry ninety percent of the maintenance load! Another third carries ten percent, the remaining third ... nothing! This is not only a dishonor to God, but also totally unfair to the other members of the group.

There are many reasons for this apparent shirking of responsibility. Sometimes it is the result of a lack of information regarding the church's program. Sometimes it is a lack of understanding concerning the function of the church. Let me illustrate.

One lady said she did not support the local church budget, because she sent all her money to a popular radio program. Then she asked, "Don't you think that is good?"

"Does the speaker of this program have a church?" I asked.

"I suppose so," was her reply.

"He really doesn't," I said. "I've been at the headquarters and there isn't any church there." She seemed puzzled at this.

"Let's assume," I went on, "That someone gives his heart to the Lord as a result of the program and is baptized, where does he go to church?"

"Why, to our church," she readily replied.

"But if everyone felt as you do and didn't support the church, there wouldn't be any. Then what would he do? Don't you realize that when you support your local church *you are supporting* your favorite program by providing a place where converts can be brought as a result of its ministry?"

"I guess I never thought of it that way," was her reaction. "I guess I'd better change my giving habits."

Shirking responsibility usually affects the total effort of the group, sometimes it even endangers it. In team sports such as football, basketball, baseball, or soccer, each member must give a total effort to produce a winning team. In war, one soldier may endanger the lives of thousands if he refuses or fails to carry out an assignment. Surely, this principle is more important in spiritual thinking.

If any two men had a reason to shirk their responsibility, they must have been Caleb and Joshua. They *knew* what was in the land of Canaan (they had been two of the spies) and here they were wandering around in the sand for forty years! They could have bitterly condemned their fellow Israelites. But nowhere does the record show that they pulled away from the group or even refused to carry their share of the burden, even their share of its guilt. But they were the *only ones* of all those adult people who went into the promised land! What a lesson this should be for us—on the borders of the heavenly Canaan.

Responsibility implies accountability.

"So then every one of us shall give account of himself to God" (Rom. 14:12). Jesus illustrated this principle in the parable of the talents. Not only were the men entrusted with their master's goods but they were also called to give an account of their use of them. Those who had been faithful, regardless of the amount involved, received the same commendation. Only the man who did nothing was condemned. We must never get the idea that responsibility is limited to us. God also possesses this attribute. He has made Himself responsible for our daily needs. "Your heavenly Father knoweth ye have need of these things" (Matt. 6:32).

He has made Himself responsible for our salvation. "He is faithful and just to forgive us our sins, and to cleanse us from all unrighteousness" (I John 1:9). He gave us His only Son that through Him we might have eternal life.

Jesus felt a responsibility for us when He willingly gave His life for us. "For when we were yet without strength, in due time Christ died for the ungodly. For scarcely for a righteous man will one die … But God commendeth his love toward us, in that, while we were yet sinners, Christ died for us" (Rom. 5:6–8).

The key to responsibility is love—love for God with corresponding love for our fellow men. This is the Christian concept in action. This is love in action … and love in action is responsibility.

Motivation

It is said that the best way to motivate a donkey is to hold a carrot in front of him and use a stick behind!

This may be a humorous solution to an age-old problem, but some type of motivation is essential to produce any activity. Millions of dollars are spent annually to get people to do things—to buy things—or to believe things. The usual methods employed are the *carrot* of desire for pay, advancement, reward or security—or the *stick* of discipline, compulsion, or insecurity.

In political campaigns the carrot and stick approach are standard procedures used to get people to vote for the right (?)

candidate. People are bombarded with speeches extolling the benefits (carrots) which will accrue if one man is elected—and the dire results (sticks) if his opponent wins.

But these are low-level motivators and at best only produce low-level results. Sometimes they even produce negative results.

I recall working on a construction job in the days when it was an employer's market. (Jobs weren't easy to get). The foreman, trying to get a little extra effort from the men, threatened to "fire" them if he didn't see more work done. As far as I could see, none of the men were lying down on the job and this threat irritated them. The actual result of this threat (stick) was a slow-down in production. Low-level motivators can do strange things.

Motivation has always been a mystery. Time, place, background, emotions, etc., all affect it. What may work today may not work tomorrow; what may work in one place may not work in another. One type of motivation may work on an individual or group one time, but fail if repeated.

One so-called expert confessed that he didn't know anything about motivation—only how to write books about it! No doubt this "confession" was based on the fact that no sure-fire method has ever been found that will guarantee a positive response in every situation.

A person's basic needs have variously been listed as (1) personal comforts, (2) security, (3) social needs, (4) ego satisfaction, (5) attaining one's goals. But these are results rather than true motivators.

It is generally agreed that to give top-level performance, a person must have an inner drive, that true motivation comes from within, rather than from without. Because, although most people respond in some degree to a desire for the so-called basic needs— the desire to accomplish something, to conquer something, or to acquire something, can be so strong that it will dwarf all considerations of creature comfort. Such a motivated individual will forego sleep or food to satisfy it.

The life stories of inventors, scientists, and explorers provide ample support for this premise. One explorer, being interviewed following an expedition in which one of his party plunged to his death, was asked why he climbed mountains when there was so much risk. His reply was simply, "Because they are there!" When asked if he would still take this chance if he knew he might lose his own life, the answer was, "Yes, even if it cost me my life."

Desire, then, can be so strong that it becomes an end in itself. Misers have starved to death in hovels where enough money was hoarded to buy a restaurant, or even a chain of them. This inner motivation can become so intense that it borders on insanity.

Motivation is essential to Christian activity but this must never be of the carrot-and-stick variety, or even self-impelled. True Christian motivation is a force unknown to human reasoning and in this sense is a complete mystery.

Jesus was, of course, the perfect example of efficient motivation. He never manipulated anyone, but He used every means to motivate them.

For example, Peter loved to fish. Jesus knew this and could have said, "Now, Peter, you're going to have to give up this fishing business—after all, we have more important work to do." But He didn't. He said, "Peter, follow me and I will make you a fisher of men!"

What an appeal to a fisherman! *Big* fish has always been the aim of all fishermen—often their arms aren't long enough to show how large the fish they caught really was! Here was an irresistible appeal.

To the woman at the well, Jesus said, "I can give you water and you will never thirst again."

"Oh, please, Sir," she pleaded, "give me this water so I won't have to come here to draw."

Every day this woman had to make the long trip from Sychar to Jacob's well—go down the many steps leading to the well—draw the water—and carry the heavy jug back up the hill. The thirst-free water Jesus promised would save her so much hard work, such a long trip each day.

But when she really understood what Jesus meant, *she left her jug* and hurried home to the village where she said, "Come see a man who told me everything I ever did ... is not this the Christ?" True motivation can make people forget their jugs!

Jesus might have said to Nicodemus, "Now, Nicodemus, you are a rich man (he was said to be one of the wealthiest in Jerusalem) because God has blessed you. I am a poor man (He didn't even own a bed) and have the Good News to give to the whole world, and this is going to take a lot of money. Now, Nicodemus, if you will make a large pledge I will put your name at the top of the list of donors, and when people see how much you have given, it will impress them to give, too. I might even find some folks who will *match* (or even double what you give." But He didn't.

Jesus quietly said, "Except a man be born again...." That little seed planted in the heart of this rich Pharisee lay dormant until he saw Jesus hanging on the cross, then it bore fruit. The record says that he gave *every bit* of his wealth to forward the work of the early church and died a poor man! What an example of fund-raising, what an example of motivation!

The key to the mystery of Christian motivation is this "born-again" experience. Peter left his nets and went after bigger game. The Samaritan woman stirred up a whole village. Nicodemus found an infinitely greater goal in life than money.

In today's Christian community we desire results and rightly so but too often we use low-level motivators which result in low-level results.

For example, GOALS are necessary to any successful program, but they are very poor motivators.

I was visiting a church one Sabbath when a large goal chart was brought out. It was in the form of a giant thermometer with the red mercury almost to the top. There was a large amount printed across the top. A man spent several minutes urging the people to "lift" ... "to get under the load" ... "to really dig down" ... but he never said what the objective might be.

My curiosity got the better of me, so I whispered to the man sitting next to me, "Why are you raising money?"

He whispered back, *"To reach the goal."*

I never did find out what it was. I forgot to ask at the close of the service.

The odometer on my car tells me how far I have come which gives me an idea as to how far I still have to go to reach my destination, but it certainly doesn't motivate me to go anywhere! Likewise, a goal is an indicator of need and progress, but a low-level motivator.

PROGRAMS are necessary to properly direct and utilize the results of proper motivation. If people are truly motivated, they will willingly give of their time, talents and means. These will require proper direction. Programs distill these into useful channels, but programs are poor motivators and possibly this is the reason for the short lives of many of them.

STATISTICS are useless as motivators except in an extremely limited way. Praising one group and shaming another never seems to affect the proportionate progress of either. If I want my dog to do something, I never tell him he is a "bad dog." If I do this, I can't even get him to come out of his house! People react in a similar way. Statistics can be valuable as progress reports but should never be used as comparisons. They produce negative reactions.

It is recognized that top-level motivation must come from within an individual, that each person has within himself a motivating force, if it can be aroused.

One popular self-improvement program advertises that deep within each individual is a diamond waiting to be mined, cut, and polished. This diamond is said to be the key to personal success. But this is not true in Christian motivation. While the force that properly motivates a Christian must come from within, it is not self-contained nor self-produced. It is the result of another power which takes control of the thoughts and actions. This is referred to as the new heart experience, a born-again situation. A person becomes a *new* being, not an old mine with a diamond inside.

A plant has no power within itself but draws its life through its roots—so the Christian draws his new life from the roots of his deep affection for Christ. His old self, his desires and affections are replaced by the desires and aspirations of God. The life-giving power of God's Spirit pervades the soul and completely changes his affections and motives.

Even his thoughts are brought into harmony with God. The results are the precious fruits of the Spirit: grace, propriety, correct deportment. This Spirit will refine and elevate the entire being.

Under this motivating force, creature needs and comforts are no longer dominant. Love for God and one's neighbor become supreme motivators—the end of all desires and aspirations. This is the transforming power of true religion, the mystery of Christian motivation.

Out of the blood-stained chapters of the Scottish Reformation comes the story of James Guthrie. His father, wealthy and influential, had high aspirations for this son, whom he felt could develop into an excellent prelate in the state church. To this end, he directed the boy's education.

The lad was an excellent student and distinguished himself both in religion and philosophy.

While attending college, James met a boy named Sam Rutherford. One evening Sam invited him to attend a prayer meeting in a little reform church. It was there, he would later relate, that he found Jesus Christ.

He graduated with honors but did not become a prelate in the popular church but rather the pastor of a humble little reform church in the country. He married and settled down to a life of service to his small flock. His father was disappointed but did nothing to stand in the way of his son's conscience.

In this little community was a high commissioner who was a rascal. The leaders of the district decided to chastise him by excommunicating him from the church. They wrote the letter of excommunication and gave it to James Guthrie to read to the congregation following his Sunday sermon. His friends tried to dissuade him, for the commissioner was a favorite of the king, but his wife said, "What the Lord gives you clearness to do—that do."

He read the letter. Very soon he was arrested and thrown into the castle prison. Taken before a drunken parliament, he was asked if he wished to say anything in his own defense. He simply stated that he had always followed the practice of carrying out what he considered to be his duty; that whatever happened to him as a result was beside the point. He was sentenced to be hanged.

On Friday night he wrote seven letters and on Saturday morning he was led to the place of execution. But, as he emerged from the dark dungeon, he paused for a moment and said, "This is the day which the Lord hath made, let us be glad in it and rejoice." *On the way to the hangman!*

At that prayer meeting, he had found Jesus Christ. This encounter overrode every other consideration—even life itself.

It has been thought that the reason some people are not involved is that they are not committed—but this is not so. The reason they are not involved is because they *are* committed, but to the wrong things. In this world there are too many things to which one can become committed.

The real reason people are not properly motivated and thus involved is because they are not converted. When one is converted, he will be committed to Jesus Christ—*he won't be able to avoid involvement.*

There are problems in the church today, such as witnessing, church maintenance, and mission outreach. Too often low-level motivators are used (carrots and sticks) when what is really needed is conversion. This is why Jesus said, "Except a man be born again." To be truly motivated a person must have this "born-again" experience for it is axiomatic that a person will support anything he believes in, *regardless of the cost!*

The Apostle Paul is a classic example of the two kinds of top-level motivation: the motivation of the world and Christian motivation.

His zeal to exterminate all Christians knew no bounds. This desire was so dominant that he could hold the coats of the men who stoned Stephen and enjoy the spectacle. Then ... he met Jesus Christ. Terrified, he asked, "Lord, what wilt thou have me to do?"

Now his zeal to bring a knowledge of Christ to the whole world was so strong he could suffer beatings, shipwreck, hunger, cold, rejection and, finally, death. He accounts for this change by saying, "For the love of Christ constraineth us (or controls) now" (II Cor. 5:14). He was now under the control of God—not Paul!

When a person completely surrenders his life to God (without any reservations) he is brought under divine control. Every thought and act comes into harmony with God's wishes. He is a new creature. This is not the result of some self-contained force, some inherent quality, but the result of an infilling of the Holy Spirit, instructing, guiding, directing.

Basic needs such as creature comforts, security, social instincts or even attaining one's life's goals are no longer a compelling force. Love for God is the top-level motivator and this is so abundant that it spills over into a consuming love for his fellow man. This becomes an end to all his goals and aspirations. This is the mystery of Christian motivation.

Procrastination

Someone has said that the only advantage to putting off until tomorrow the things which should be done today is that tomorrow may never come.

I can't say that I was overjoyed at the prospect of waiting around in the Los Angeles airport four hours for a jet which would take me to Chicago, but I found my way down a long concourse to the loading gate, took a comfortable seat, and settled down with a book.

I was seated directly across from where an agent was busily processing the tickets of some departing passengers. I could see their plane parked just outside the terminal.

I had barely started to read when I heard echoes of laughing and talking growing louder and louder. Looking down the concourse, I saw a group of people come around a corner. There must have been thirty or thirty-five and they were certainly enjoying themselves.

I laid the book aside and began trying to figure out what it was all about. It didn't take too long. There were two ladies leading the procession, all dressed up—hats, gloves, corsages—who were obviously the reason for the celebration. From bits of conversation I managed to sort out from all the laughing, I gathered that these two ladies were going to New York where Uncle Joe was to meet them at Kennedy Airport. (Aunt Louise was going to get a hug and a kiss from someone.) The rest of the group were relatives and friends come to see them off.

As they approached the podium, the agent said, "Could I have your tickets, please?" Without a break in the conversation, they pawed around in their handbags, found the tickets, and handed them to him. He checked them, removed the right one, and handed them back with a pleasant, "You can board now. Have a pleasant trip."

The tickets disappeared in the bags and they went right on talking. I began to worry. I had already seen the copilot complete his routine check of the outside of the aircraft. Now I could see him through the window of the cockpit checking gauges and instruments. Everyone else was on board, but this group just went on talking and laughing.

Finally, to my consternation, they drifted into the waiting area and began to sit down. I wondered if I should say something to them. (They would probably tell me to mind my own business.) Should I say something to the agent? (He was occupied with his work.) So ... I did nothing, except worry.

Soon I heard the whine of an engine as it came to life, then another. The long accordion jetway was being retracted and the door closed; the great ship was being shoved out of the loading gate.

The tractor had been disconnected and the plane was turning toward the runway when someone in the group happened to look out the window. I never saw such commotion—more than thirty people trying to go in eight directions at the same time. They converged on the hapless agent, all talking at the same time. "You've got to stop the plane! Uncle Joe! Aunt Louise! The luggage! You have to stop the plane!" They buried the poor fellow under an avalanche of words.

He stood there utterly confused trying to figure out what was happening. Then, he saw the two ladies! His mouth opened but the words wouldn't come out. "Y-y-y-you? ... Y-y-y-you aren't on board? B-b-b-b-but I said you could board. I thought you were on board."

"You have to stop the plane! You've got to!"

"I can't—it's too late."

"But you have to ... our luggage ... Uncle Joe ...what are we going to do?" Efficiency took over. Quieting them with a gesture, he told them to wait a minute. He picked up the phone and talked for a little while, then asked for their tickets and said he had confirmed reservations for another flight which would leave *two hours later!*

He directed them to another loading area and they headed back down the concourse. I watched as they passed—the quietest, most subdued group of people I have ever seen. Not a word. No laughter. Nothing. All the anticipation—all the joy of the departure was gone. Gone.

My book lay unopened for some time as I thought over the scene I had witnessed and drew my own lesson from it.

We use two words to indicate a delay in making a decision or in taking some action. One word is deliberation, the other procrastination.

Deliberation implies that we need more information, or further study regarding the methods to be used, or possibly some alternate plan. However, deliberation indicates a desire to make a decision to take some action; the delay is only that we may secure a more favorable result.

Procrastination, on the other hand, is the result of a desire to avoid, or delay taking some action or making some decision. In this situation the action or decision does not require any further study—the time element is NOW. Notice some threadbare excuses often used.

"I just don't feel like it."

"I'll get up earlier tomorrow."

"I'll do it later."

'I'm going to wait until I'm in a better mood."

What are the reasons for procrastination outside of indolence?

Too many projects are planned for the time available. One may get into the habit of crisis living—depending on someone or something to bail him out at the last minute.

Often wrong attitudes toward a task can be the contributing factor. Duties are being regarded as pleasant or unpleasant, rather than necessary or unnecessary.

However, whatever the reasons, there are undesirable results from procrastination.

First. It may "jam" the calendar. Duties left until tomorrow will occupy the time required for tomorrow's requirements. Second. It may be costly. Neglect to repair the roof can result in a damaged interior and/or ruined furniture. Improper car maintenance can result in costly repairs. Third. There is a certain loss of self-respect, not only for ourselves, but also the respect of those who may be affected by our actions.

There is a fourth and more serious result of procrastination.

IF THE DEVIL CAN GET US INTO THE HABIT OF PUTTING OFF THE THINGS IN OUR DAILY LIVES WHICH SHOULD BE DONE PROMPTLY—THIS SAME HABIT MAY CAUSE US TO POSTPONE OUR SPIRITUAL PREPARATION, UNTIL IT IS FOREVER TOO LATE.

Consider how procrastination affected these people:

The foolish virgins in the parable simply "put off" getting sufficient oil for their lamps. It was available. They just didn't get it.

The Roman governor, Felix, called for the prisoner Paul one day and listened intently as Paul "reasoned of righteousness, temperance and judgment to come." He trembled, and said to Paul, "Go thy way for this time; when I have a *more convenient season*, I will call for thee" (Acts 24:25; Italics supplied). That *convenient* season never came.

Through procrastination, Pilate lost control of the situation. He could have examined Jesus, declared Him innocent, and released Him, and then had his soldiers disperse the Jews. *Three times* he said, "I find no fault in this man." Then, by delaying his decision, his job was on the line. For the Jewish leaders said, "If thou let this man go, thou art not Caesar's friend." And this was a reputation he couldn't afford.

Procrastination is a violation of the *stewardship of time*. Time is the most valuable thing a man has, for it is the essence of life. One cannot borrow one second from tomorrow nor recall one second from yesterday. Each person has been given enough time for the essential tasks of daily living and for his spiritual preparation.

But too often the devil is successful in getting one to delay his spiritual preparation by either the neglect of present duties or by making material interests seem all-important.

One day I climbed the broad steps leading up to the Cairo museum. Just as I approached the door, a man blocked my way with the declaration, "Sir, you need a guide."

"Not really," I replied.

"Yes, sir," he insisted, "you need a guide."

I really didn't think I needed a guide to tour the museum, but I soon came to the conclusion that if I was going to see anything except this Arab's face, possibly I did, for no matter which way I turned, he seemed to be there. So we began negotiations about a price for his "indispensable" services.

I was soon caught up in the vastness of this beautiful building and the seemingly endless displays of gold, silver, and alabaster artifacts. I saw gold chairs, tables, bedsteads, chariots. Intricate carvings sparkling with gems dazzled my eyes. This was indeed the fortune of a king.

I hesitated before one unusual display. "Would you like to take a picture?" my guide suggested.

"Well, it would be nice—but…" I spread my hands in a helpless gesture for many tourists blocked the way.

"No problem," was his reply as he opened a pathway with a wave of his hands and a "please, madam, please, sir." I took the picture as quickly as possible and said, "Thank you," but no one said I was welcome.

Gradually, the thought began to creep into my mind that here was a display of such magnitude that it was unreal. I turned to my guide and said, "Old King Tut certainly made a lot of preparation for the future life, didn't he?"

He thought about this for a minute, then said, "You wouldn't understand this, sir, but you see the king felt that there was so much of the next life and so little of this one, that *he should spend all of this one just preparing for the next one!*"

I took him by the hand and said, "Thank you, my friend … thank you."

I needed that guide, I really did, and the generous tip I gave him expressed my gratitude for a lesson never forgotten.

An attitude such as this would place the relationship between material needs and spiritual preparation in true perspective.

There are some principles which will help a person avoid procrastination or take corrective steps to overcome it.

MAKE A LIST (written or mental). Advance planning is necessary for an efficient program. Realistic goals should be set for the time available. Priorities must be established.

START EARLY. Nothing is so detrimental to a day's program as getting started too late. "Awake with nature and the early-rising birds" is wise counsel. One man was advised to get up while the "stars were still shining."

COMPLETE EACH TASK. Wherever it is possible, each task should be completed. Being surrounded by unfinished work can be very frustrating.

MAINTAIN THE RIGHT ATTITUDE. Instead of regarding work as pleasant or unpleasant, think of it as necessary or unnecessary (essential or nonessential). Remember that anything that *needs* to be done is honorable work and should be done with dispatch and a cheerful attitude.

A word of caution is in order. Don't become a slave to your plans. If you "run out of steam" before all the jobs you have planned have been completed, STOP! It is far better to leave some things undone than to use up the energy and courage needed for the following day to complete them. One must never violate the laws of nature for the sake of adhering to some schedule.

To avoid spiritual procrastination one must obey God's requirements *without any hesitation.* Twice the Israelites could have gone into the promised land *if* they had moved when God directed. Twice they *waited* until the next day, but by then it was too late and they suffered defeat. Putting off until tomorrow the things that should be done today i   s always dangerous. "For thou knowest not what a day may bring forth" (Prov. 27:1).

I heard that a former college friend of mine was living in a small city I was planning to pass through. After doing some checking, I finally contacted him, and what a happy reunion it was. Over lunch we brought each other up to date on the years that had passed since we last saw each other.

Because of the nature of his work, I naturally wondered about his affiliation with the church. So, at a point in our conversation which I felt would be appropriate, I asked him.

He was thoughtful for a moment, then said, "No—I don't belong to the church any more. You see, I sort of drifted away for a while. I met this lovely girl and we were married. The family came along, and with my work and all—well, I never got around to coming back. You know how it is."

He paused, then went on, "Oh, I've often thought about it—in fact, I intend to do it—I really do. But ... well, I'm not sure my wife and family would understand ... and she's a wonderful wife and mother. B-b-but you don't know how trapped I feel sometimes." His face had a trapped look.

I spoke to him seriously about putting off his decision and he assured me again and again that he was going to do something about it—*right away.*

My work took me to that city frequently after that and I always dropped by to see him. To my question, he always gave the same answer, "No, not yet—but I'm going to ... probably by your next trip."

He made a few half-hearted attempts but never really made a break. When he attended church, it was always as a visitor. He and his wife visited me at my motel one evening and she was such a lovely person that I was never convinced that she wouldn't have understood if he had followed his convictions. But I'll never know.

Another worker in our office dropped by one Monday morning and said he had just returned from this area of the state. "By the way," he remarked as he was leaving, "I heard a friend of yours passed away down there." Somehow I sensed the answer before I asked the question. *He died on his way to work one morning.* I can still hear him say, "I'm going to do it—you'll see—probably by your next trip." But he waited too long.

In the little William Miller chapel in Low Hampton, New York, there is a motto on the wall behind the pulpit taken from Daniel 8:19, "For at the *time appointed* the end shall be" (Italics supplied). Paul warned, "Behold, *now* is the accepted time; behold, *now* is the day of salvation" (II Cor. 6:2; Italics supplied).

As my Egyptian guide would say, there is so much of the next life and so little of this one—we should spend all of this one just getting ready for the next one.

One day soon, Jesus is coming with all the holy angels. There will be a great white cloud on which we will be carried to the realms of glory. It is so important that we be on that cloud—for there isn't going to be another leaving ... *two hours later!*

TEACH Services, Inc.
P U B L I S H I N G

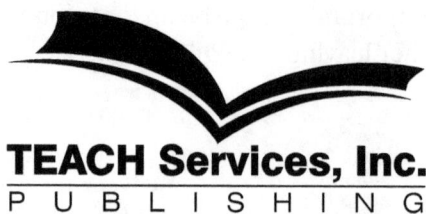

We invite you to view the complete
selection of titles we publish at:
www.TEACHServices.com

We encourage you to write us
with your thoughts about this,
or any other book we publish at:
info@TEACHServices.com

TEACH Services' titles may be purchased in
bulk quantities for educational, fund-raising,
business, or promotional use.
bulksales@TEACHServices.com

Finally, if you are interested in seeing
your own book in print, please contact us at:
publishing@TEACHServices.com

We are happy to review your manuscript at no charge.

www.ingramcontent.com/pod-product-compliance
Lightning Source LLC
Chambersburg PA
CBHW060552100426
42742CB00013B/2524